The Egyptian Bourse

Compiled and edited by Sherif Boraïe and Boutros Boutros Ghali.
Additional research and captions by Ola Seif.

Plates are from the collections of Boutros Boutros Ghali, Sherif Raafat, Ola Seif and Sherif Boraïe.
Plate of *Compagnie Universelle du Canal Maritime de Suez* courtesy of Khaled el Tawil.

First published in Egypt by Zeitouna
30 Abdine Square, Cairo, Egypt 11111
admin@zeitouna.com

ISBN 977 5864 16 X
Dar el Kotob 22442/2010

Printed in Egypt

The Egyptian Bourse

Samir Raafat

Forewords by

HH Prince Abbas Hilmi

&

HE Youssef Boutros Ghali

Zeitouna

HH Prince Abbas Hilmi

The Stock Market is a mirror of the economy and, to a large extent, of the society to which it belongs.

Samir Raafat describes vividly how from fairly modest beginnings at the end of the nineteenth century, the Cairo Stock Exchange blossomed for most of the first half of twentieth century.

The turn of these two centuries was a particularly important period in modern Egyptian history. Thanks to the much maligned debt it had accumulated during the reign of Khedive Ismail, Egypt was endowed with a good infrastructure of roads, railways, bridges and irrigation canals. During the reign of Khedive Tewfik, Ismail's son, and in an unique example of duty towards their country, the Royal family secured the national debt with their own possessions, the Daira Saniya. The State then proceeded to sell those holdings and repay the national debt. This coincided with a robust recovery in the price of cotton which was Egypt's main export commodity. As a result of these two combined factors, the economy took off.

All sorts of companies were formed: industrial, development and transport companies, banks and the like. Many turned to the Stock Exchange to raise capital.

In this atmosphere of prosperity during the reign of Khedive Abbas Hilmi II, the country saw a tremendous cultural activity with poets such as Ahmed Shawky, El Baroudy and many others. The Opera house thrived in Cairo and in Alexandria, Oriental music reached its peak, and tourists flocked to Egypt in ever increasing numbers.

Gazettes proliferated and political activity became very important with the rise of many thinkers like Sheikh Mohamed Abdu and nationalist politicians like Moustafa Kamel, founder of the National Party. Egypt attracted people such as Kamal El Din El Afghany who had been forced to leave his native Afghanistan and became a leader in Egypt.

Likewise, the Cairo Stock Exchange became one of the leading exchanges in the world. It quoted companies in Egyptian Pounds as well as Pounds Sterling, Swiss Francs, French Francs, Belgian Francs and U.S. Dollars. Many companies quoted in Cairo were also quoted in London, Paris, Brussels, Geneva and New York.

Cairo became a regional financial centre with companies such as the Palestine Potash Company quoted in Cairo. The Cairo Stock Exchange was international and very sophisticated, with for example The Egyptian Enterprise and Development Company floating a "Deferred Share Warrant to Bearer".

The story of the Cairo Stock Exchange needed to be told and I congratulate the editor, Sherif Boraïe, for this excellent book where he managed to get such a distinguished list of contributors.

Cairo 26/10/2010

HE Youssef Boutros-Ghali

The past glory of Egypt is not limited to its faraway history and civilization. The greatness of thousands of years was there less than one hundred years ago.

An economic power, a financial center, and a thriving civil society were all there in the early twenties and thirties. And if today Egypt is working at restoring its past glory, we should not forget the days of greatness a few decades ago.

This book brings back in vivid detail those days. It is a tribute to our economic history and guide to what we can become again.

Cairo 24/11/2010

During one of their turn-of-the-century meetings at the Cafe New Bar, Cairo's merchants and brokers were once again reminded by Monsieur Moise Cattaui the time had come for Cairo to follow Alexandria's example and have its own bourse.

A pillar of the business community, Cattaui pointed out that the number of limited liability companies had reached seventy-nine with an aggregate capital of 29 million pounds. The city's taipans could no longer conduct pork-barrel politics on Cairo sidewalks or inside its coffee shops and hotels.

A board of directors was elected. Temporarily the job of board secretary went to Monsieur Botini. The founding directors included representatives from the principal banks operating in Egypt: Credit Lyonnais, the Ottoman Bank, the National Bank, Banque d'Égypte and the Anglo Bank. The remaining two directors representing the commodity and cereal markets were Adolphe Cattaui and Monsieur Mortera. The job of president of the board naturally went to Moise Cattaui Bey.

And so it was on Thursday, 21 May 1903 that an ad hoc site committee, presided by Cattaui Bey, chose the Manuk Building, which had once hosted the Ottoman Bank (today Groppi-Adly Branch) on Maghrabi Street, as the temporary official headquarters of the newly incorporated Bourse and Banking Company of Egypt Limited a.k.a. Bourse Khediviale du Caire.

With ambitious plans in mind, the new company leased the premises for a non-renewable period of six years at an annual rent of 400 pounds. In the meantime, an international competition was initiated for the design of a dedicated bourse to be situated at the center of Cairo's European district of Ismailia, not far from the National Bank of Egypt (today the Central Bank).

The prize for best design went in April 1907 to French award-winning architect Raoul Brandon who had recently designed Cairo's Orosdi-Back/Omar Effendi department store on Abdel Aziz Street.

The timing couldn't have been better, or so everyone thought. Emboldened by success and drunk on growth, the promoters of Cairo's bourse were in an excessive mood. It was public knowledge that lumped together the Cairo and Alexandria Bourses rated among the world's top five Stock Exchanges.

Egypt's economy was at an all-time high and the number of companies traded in the Cairo Bourse alone had reached 228 with a combined capital of 91 million pounds. Seventy-three brokers and intermediaries were on hand to take care of the spiraling share trading. The modest premises on Maghrabi Street had most certainly outlived its usefulness. It was time for swank.

Swank yes, but like the swing of a pendulum, the high state of euphoria disappeared overnight. Prudence having given way to high-risk speculation, what had started out with a real estate boom in Egypt ended in what became known in the annals of speculative history as the Crash of 1907.

Société du Cercle Mohamed Aly

Founded in Alexandria in 1888.

Capital: £3600 divided into 720 shares of £5 each.

Lst 5

Lst 5

SOCIÉTÉ DU CERCLE MOHAMMED ALY

N° [illegible]

Société du Cercle Mohammed-Aly

Capital Lst. 3,600.

Une part de Propriété de Cinq Livres Sterling

delivrée au nom de Monsieur M. Pondi...

Lst. 5.

ALEXANDRIE, Avril ...

Un Membre du Comité: A. Simons

Le Secrétaire tresorier: ...

SOCIÉTÉ DU CERCLE MOHAMMED ALY

Propriété Cercle Mohammed Aly

ANNULÉ

Extrait des Statuts

Art. 5. — Le Capital est divisé en **sept cent vingt parts de Livres Sterling cinq** chaque, dénommées parts de propriété et donnant droit chacune à un tantième de l'actif social et de ses produits. Les souscripteurs ne sont engagés que jusqu'à concurrence du montant de leur souscription.

Art. 6. — Les parts de propriété seront nominatives. La cession ne pourra avoir lieu que par voie de transfert et au profit d'un membre du Cercle. Le transfert, signé par le membre de la Société désigné à cet effet, sera inscrit sur le titre et mentionné sur un registre *ad hoc* au Secrétariat du Cercle Mohammed-Aly.

Art. 7. — En cas de décès ou de démission, les ayants droit ou porteurs de parts de propriété seront tenus de vendre les dites parts, et ne pourront les vendre qu'à un membre du Cercle et ce dans le délai d'un an au plus, sous peine d'annulation de leurs parts au profit de la Caisse Sociale.

Some misguided historians concede the panic of 1907 began in Alexandria with the failure in July of Cassa di Sconto. Japan was hit next, then Germany, then Chile. By October, the fallout had reached Europe and the United States. Back home, several over-extended banks folded. As share prices plummeted, a now jobless broker, Mr. Alfred Nahman, was appointed chief liquidator of the Bourse and Banking Company of Egypt Limited.

Eighteen months after Brandon's publicized award to build the Bourse building that never was, the Corporation of Agents de Change commissioned the Cairo firm of Edward Matasek and Maurice J. Cattaui, with the participation of Ernest Jaspar, to design and erect an Exchange Building.

Adorned with Matasek's trademark accouterments of Hermes busts and ornate stucco, the resultant edifice was the handsomest building on the block. At long last Cairo had a real trading floor with a high gallery from where share trading could be observed by the concerned public. Over the years, the building, which stands opposite the French consulate, was occupied by Lloyds Bank, the British Chamber of Commerce, the National Bank of Egypt and now by the Watany Development Bank.

Trading had hardly started on 30 April 1909 at Sharia al-Borsa al-Gedida (New Bourse Street) when it was announced that Egypt's leading laissez-faire banker-industrialist Raphael Suarès had died. The bourse closed for the rest of the day. It was largely thanks to his efforts that Cairo had a bourse in the first place. In view of his untimely death, Suarès missed by a few months the imposition of the first ever bourse regulations.

On 7 June 1927, the Societe Anonyme de l'Immeuble de la Bourse du Caire was launched with an initial issue of 4,000 shares worth LE 5 each. The purpose was the purchase of a plot of land and the subsequent construction of a new bourse building.

Because he had died in 1924, Moise Cattaui, the original promoter of the Cairo Bourse who had been elevated to a pasha, had no way of knowing that four years after his departure the bourse would relocate on part of what had once been his Cairo palace. In its heyday, Palais Cattaui extended from the National Bank of Egypt all the way to Midan Soliman Pasha (now Talaat Harb). As though a reminder for his capital efforts, the Cairo Bourse is to this day flanked by two side streets, one of them named after Moussa (Moise) Cattaui.

It was in 1928, a year before the Wall Street crash, that the revitalized Cairo Bourse moved into its present premises on Cherifein Street. The neo-classic building with its multiple ionic colonnades is the work of French architect George Parcq who was responsible for much of Cairo's elegant interwar buildings including Sednaoui's department store on Midan Khazindar. Coincidence perhaps, for the site on which Sednaoui was built had once been the first meeting place for Cairo's speculative traders prior to the formation of Cairo's first bourse.

Before it was nationalized in July 1961 following the state-sanctioned demise of Egypt's private sector, the Cairo and Alexandria Bourse (they had already merged) was listed fourth in the world.

Industrial Building Company of Egypt

Founded in 1908, the Industrial Building Company of Egypt was specialized in constructing factory premises in Alexandria. Unlike many companies, it was registered at the Alexandria Mixed Tribunal, evidence of its diversified international clientele.

The unique art nouveau graphic design, an anomaly to Egyptian stock certificates, is reminiscient of contemporaneous French stocks such as the 1906 Brouhot car factory, and Guimard's art nouveau touches of cast iron at the entrances of the Parisian Metropolitan metros at the turn of the century. A discreet Egyptian touch — the typical pharaonic eagled ornamental crown — graces the head of the semi-nude.

By 1938, the company had been liquidated.

Capital:
Founded in 1908 with the capital of £200,000 divided into 50,000 shares of £4 each.

INDUSTRIAL BUILDING COMPANY OF EGYPT

ACTIONS 5 | ACTIONS 5

ACTIONS 5 | ACTIONS 5

INDVSTRIA

LABOR

SOCIÉTÉ ANONYME

CRÉÉE PAR DÉCRET KHÉDIVIAL
du 3 Juillet 1908.

Statuts déposés au Greffe Commercial du Tribunal
Mixte d'Alexandrie le 29 Juillet 1908
sub N° 997.

TITRE N° 6818 AU PORTEUR

DE CINQ ACTIONS DE QUATRE LIVRES STERLING
CHACUNE
ENTIÈREMENT LIBÉRÉES

N° DES ACTIONS DE 14086 À 14090

Alexandrie le 1 Janvier 1912

DEUX ADMINISTRATEURS

CAPITAL SOCIAL
Lstg. 200.000
DIVISÉ EN 50.000 ACTIONS DE Lstg. 4 CHACUNE
CAPITAL EMIS ET VERSÉ
Lstg. 150.000

LITH. G. ASPIOTIS FRÈRES-CORFOU

The rise and fall of Alexandria's Cotton Exchange

Alexandria's Futures Market is one of the oldest in the world. The first locally-recorded cotton transaction took place in 1865 in Alexandria's Café de l'Europe on Place des Consuls which was later renamed Mohammed Ali Square. It was there that cotton merchants met and cut deals based on supply and demand for the long staple Karnak and Menouf or the short to medium staple Ashmouni, Giza and Zagora. Over the years, deals extended to cotton seed varieties such as Hull, Afifi and Sakellaridis.

The first cotton deal-makers eagerly awaited the weekly arrival of the news-sheets from Europe to guide future operations. Reputation counted for everything. Cotton growers who delivered on time were courted by exporters and received large orders the following season. Timing and reliability were of the essence if profits were to be made.

From Café de l'Europe, cotton deal-makers moved to a nearby building. As business grew, the Association Cottoniere d'Alexandrie (later the Alexandria General Produce Association or AGPA) was created for the purpose of trading in cotton, cotton seeds and cereals in the spot and future markets.

In 1899, during the reign of Khedive Abbas Hilmi II, AGPA moved to an imposing new building henceforth called The Bourse. Situated on Mohammed Ali Square, the Alexandria Bourse quickly became a city landmark featured on postcards, books and city guides. In more ways than one, the Bourse was the focal point of the city's financial community. Meanwhile, the Association's old offices were transformed into a bank, and later into the Top Hat night club.

In 1909, cotton forward contracts were legalized to coincide with Egypt's recovery from a massive economic slump brought on by the financial crash of 1907 when banking and real estate institutions collapsed due to excessive speculation. So far, government intervention had been practically absent and the spot market of Minet al-Bassal would be left alone until 1931.

Of the 35 registered cotton brokers in 1950, only two were Egyptian. Likewise, the directors of the Alexandria Bourse were an uneven mixture of Egyptians, Levantines and Jews. Its veteran president was Jules Klat Bey from Syria. Despite its ethnic mixture, AGPA had come a long way since Britons controlled it through two of Alexandria's largest cotton exporters, the Carver and Moss families. And when a Carver scion married the Moss heiress, they held an even stronger grip on this lucrative export market.

Likewise, cotton ginning mills were controlled in great part by foreigners foremost among them were Selig Kusel from Manchester, the Plantas from Liverpool, the Lindemanns from Prague and Dresden, and the Choremi-Benachi-Salvagos representing the Greek connection. One of the few pre-1900 Egyptian-owned cotton mills was that which belonged to Amin Chamsi Pasha of Sharkia where a Kusel family member had once apprenticed.

Bourse des Marchandises d'Alexandrie

A loan of L.E. 75,000 issued in 1942 by the Alexandria Bourse of Commodities to lend funds to brokers and middlemen after its closure due to the War.

١٠ جنيه مصرى

10 L. EG.

بورصة البضائع بالاسكندرية

BOURSE DES MARCHANDISES D'ALEXANDRIE

EMPRUNT DE L. E. 75.000

Émis par la Commission de la Bourse des Marchandises d'Alexandrie en vertu et en conformité du décret du 7 Avril 1941 et de l'arrêté Ministériel du 8 Août 1942.

Affecté à des avances aux courtiers, remisiers et jobbers, en conséquence de la situation créée par suite de la fermeture de la Bourse.

قرض بمبلغ ٧٥٫٠٠٠ جنيه مصرى صادر من لجنة بورصة البضائع بالاسكندرية بمقتضى مرسوم ٧ ابريل سنة ١٩٤١ وطبقاً لاحكامه والقرار الوزارى الصادر فى ٨ اغسطس سنة ١٩٤٢

هذا القرض مخصص لسلفيات الى السماسرة والوسطاء والمياومين بسبب الحالة الناشئة عن تعطيل البورصة .

SÉRIE A N° 1041

مجموعة حرف ا رقم ١٠٤١

BON AU PORTEUR

DE L. E. 10

(Dix Livres Egyptiennes)

productif d'intérêts cumulatifs de cinq pour cent à partir du 1er Septembre 1942.

Alexandrie, le 1er Septembre 1942.

اذن لحامله

بمبلغ ١٠ جنيه مصرى

(عشرة جنيه مصرى)

بفوائد متراكمة قيمتها ٥ ٪ ابتداء من اول سبتمبر سنة ١٩٤٢

الاسكندرية فى اول سبتمبر سنة ١٩٤٢

LE PRÉSIDENT DE LA COMMISSION DE LA BOURSE DES MARCHANDISES,

رئيس لجنة بورصة البضائع

LE TRÉSORIER,

امين الصندوق

SOCIÉTÉ DE PUBLICATIONS EGYPTIENNES - ALEX.

From the 1880s up until the 1950s, most of the trading was done with the Liverpool Cotton Exchange, evidence of Egypt's strong ties with the waning British Empire. The powerful Manchester trade relied heavily on this staple which was responsible for untold fortunes made in the UK. Not unlike oil today, Egyptian cotton trade was politicized during the interwar period figuring as a clause in most of Egypt's international agreements. It had become a major bargaining tool used as collateral for Egypt's currency.

The Joint Egyptian Cotton Committee and the Cotton Institute were two highly respected institutions affiliated with the International Cotton Congress. With time, more and more Egyptians entered the trade once the jealously-guarded preserve of the Finneys, the Rheinharts, the Rolos, the Cicurels and Pintos. Newcomers included Talaat Harb Pasha, a founder of the Banque Misr group of companies, and Mohammed Farghaly Pasha, president of the Alexandria Cotton Exporters Association. On the expert side, there was Ahmed Abdel Wahab Pasha, a former minister of finance, and Fouad Abaza Pasha, the director of the Royal Agricultural Society.

Just as the native intelligentsia was about to have its turn at the helm, agricultural trade was brought within the aegis of the state through a series of agrarian reform laws in the 1950s. Henceforth, the agricultural sector mutated into unprofitable small holdings and bureaucratic cooperatives. A few years later, the Bourse itself was nationalized by Egypt's rising strongman, Gamal Abdel Nasser. Capitalism went into rigor mortis and soon enough King Cotton suffered the same fate.

Ironically it would be from the parapet of the Alexandria Bourse that Nasser first grabbed international media attention. This took place in July 1956 during his epoch-making speech when he announced to the world that he had nationalized the Suez Canal Company. For a brief period, the Alexandria bourse building had become more than a definitive symbol of Egypt's thriving cotton-based capitalism.

Société Egyptienne de la Bourse Commerciale de Minet el Bassal

In 1884, three financiers, George Goussio, Louis H. Birch and Emmanuel Benachi formed a company to acquire from the Egyptian Government the building known as the Bourse Commerciale de Minet el-Bassal in Alexandria. The acquisition was transferred to the Société Egyptienne de la Bourse Commerciale de Minet el-Bassal, and the building became the sole exchange in Egypt where cotton and cotton-seed spot business were transacted.

Head Office: 5 Old Bourse Street, Alexandria.

Capital:
£70,000 divided into 14,000 Ordinary shares of £5 each, fully paid.

SOCIÉTÉ EGYPTIENNE DE LA BOURSE COMMERCIALE DE MINET-EL-BASSAL

Fondée suivant firman du 26 Mai 1884

SOCIÉTÉ ANONYME AU CAPITAL DE £stg. 70,000, DIVISÉ EN 14,000 ACTIONS DE £stg. 5 CHACUNE

1 ACTION

Action de Cinq Livres Sterling au Porteur

5 £stg.

Nº 00829

Alexandrie (Egypte), le 15 Février 1923

Pour le Conseil d'Administration

Un Administrateur

Un Administrateur

SOCIÉTÉ EGYPTIENNE DE LA BOURSE COMMERCIALE DE MINET-EL-BASSAL 1884

The Buy of the Century

Despite the Union Jack fluttering above 75% of the Suez Canal traffic, France was the major European player in Egypt's financial affairs. Frenchmen and French companies held majority interests in the international waterway and controlled Egypt's principal banks.

Then things changed in Britain's favor.

With Khedive Ismail on the brink of bankruptcy, his bankers — Oppenheim Alberti & Co., the Anglo-Egyptian Bank, Société General, Bischoffscheim of London and Brussels, Edouard de Vries of Paris and Andre Dervieu in Cairo — refused to extend his credit. Faced with crippling debts and a devastated economy, the Khedive resorted to an action which unwittingly ensured Egypt's subjugation to European, most notably British, imperialism.

On 25 November 1875, an epic document was signed by Ismail Sadek, Khedive Ismail's ill-fated minister of finance and General Edward Stanton, the British consul-general in Cairo. As a result, Egypt's stake in the Suez Canal Company amounting to 176,602 shares out of a total of 400,000 ordinary shares, were signed over to His Majesty's Government against the sum of four million pounds sterling (equivalent to 27.5 million in 1979 value).

Lacking four million pounds to purchase the shares, the British treasury obtained an advance at one day notice from Baron Lionel Nathan Meyer de Rothschild. The cost of the loan to the British government was a flat commission of 2.5% plus a 5% interest charge per year. Aside from making 100,000 pounds on this momentous deal, Rothschild won the irrevocable esteem of his co-religionist and friend Prime Minister Benjamin Disraeli.

The sale of the Khedive's shares concluded, the certificates were sealed in seven large zinc boxes and deposited at the British consulate. Forty shares were found missing and later a public notary discovered two more shares were unaccounted for and two were duplicated. On 16 December 1875, the zinc boxes sailed for Portsmouth aboard the HMS Malobar. In England, they traveled by guarded escort to the Bank of England. From that day, Egypt's participation in the Canal's affairs was reduced to that of a convenience flag for the Suez Canal Company. And Great Britain was about to become a principal shareholder in the Middle East. But first, Egypt had to be secured, lock, stock and canal.

Among the major players in Egypt's destiny was a close-knit network of European Jewish bankers. Most notable among them was Baron Maurice de Hirsch (d. 1896). Although he controlled the powerful Anglo-Austrian Bank, he is best remembered for having financed the Vienna–Constantinople Railway on which the first Orient Express ran in 1888. Through business mergers and acquisitions, Hirsch was connected to most of the private Jewish banks of Europe and through marriage was related to most of their owners. One of them, Sir Ernest Cassel was a man who would have a profound impact on the development of Egypt's economy.

Compagnie Universelle du Canal Maritime de Suez

The Suez Canal Company was established by decrees of the Viceroy of Egypt on November 30, 1854 and January 5, 1856, and confirmed by the firman of the Ottoman Sultan on March 19, 1866.

The company's concession allowed for operating the Canal for 99 years from November 17, 1869 at the expiration of which the Canal would revert to the Egyptian Government.

Capital:
FF 132,0689,500 in 530,758 Ordinary bearer shares of FF 250 each, fully paid.
FF 67,310,500 in 69,242 Jouissance shares of no nominal value.
100,000 Founders bearer shares of no nominal value.

SOCIÉTÉ CIVILE

Constituée suivant acte passé devant Mes PORTEFIN et son collègue, notaires à Paris, le 17 Avril 1880,

POUR LE RECOUVREMENT DES 15 °/₀ DES PRODUITS NETS

DE LA

COMPAGNIE UNIVERSELLE DU CANAL MARITIME DE SUEZ

FONDS SOCIAL DIVISÉ EN 84.507 PARTS OU 422.535 CINQUIÈMES DE PARTS

Les Cinquièmes de Part ont été créés suivant délibération de l'Assemblée générale des Porteurs de Parts, en date du 15 Mai 1882, déposée à Me PORTEFIN.

L'échange des Parts anciennes contre des Parts nouvelles ou Cinquièmes de Parts a été rendu obligatoire suivant délibération de l'Assemblée générale des Porteurs de Parts, en date du 8 Juillet 1930, déposée au rang des minutes de Me THIBIERGE, notaire à Paris, successeur de Me PORTEFIN.

Les quinze pour cent dont les recouvrements et répartition font l'objet de la Société ont été attribués par la *Compagnie Universelle du Canal Maritime de Suez* au Gouvernement Égyptien, aux termes de l'article 63 des Statuts de ladite Société, constituée en Égypte le 5 Janvier 1856, en conformité du décret de concession rendu le même jour par Son Altesse le Vice-Roi. — Ils ont été apportés à la Société Civile par l'ayant droit du Gouvernement Égyptien avec tous les avantages y attachés dans la proportion des revenus de la Compagnie.

Le *Comptoir d'Escompte de Paris* est constitué mandataire pour toucher les quinze pour cent de produits et les répartir. Suivant délibération de l'Assemblée générale des Porteurs de Parts, en date du 18 Juillet 1889, le *Comptoir National d'Escompte de Paris* a été constitué mandataire et représentant unique de la Société Civile, en remplacement du *Comptoir d'Escompte de Paris*.

Certificat de UN CINQUIÈME de Part au Porteur

No 126,206

Le présent Certificat donne droit, jusqu'à la fin de la concession de la Compagnie Universelle du Canal Maritime de Suez *(1968), à 1/422.535me des quinze pour cent des produits nets à recevoir après l'encaissement du dividende dont les Statuts (art. 64) indiquent le paiement au 1er Juillet de chaque année.*

PARIS, LE 1er OCTOBRE 1930.

POUR LA SOCIÉTÉ CIVILE :
UN DÉLÉGUÉ DU CONSEIL DU COMPTOIR NATIONAL D'ESCOMPTE DE PARIS,
MANDATAIRE ET REPRÉSENTANT UNIQUE,
Le Président,

POUR LA SOCIÉTÉ CIVILE :
UN DÉLÉGUÉ DU CONSEIL DU COMPTOIR NATIONAL D'ESCOMPTE DE PARIS
MANDATAIRE ET REPRÉSENTANT UNIQUE,

G. FRAIPONT. INV. DEL.   A. RENARD

Privatizing the Daira Sanieh

The 1980s privatization wave in Egypt had a sense of newness about it, but close observers of the nation's history know that we've been down this road before and perhaps more boldly. The sell-off over a century ago of the Daira Sanieh, the country's largest state-run company of the 19th century, is a case in point.

In the 1870s, Khedive Ismail's private and public debts had reached £E 91 million, plunging the country into receivership. A system of "dual control" was introduced, whereby Egypt's finances were run by a joint Franco-British administration. The Khedivial estate of the Daira Sanieh, which had been used as collateral for one of the ruler's loans, was then run by a government-appointed board. After 20 years of government management under this arrangement, the Daira Sanieh was still in the red.

Everyone agreed the Daira had unlimited potential. Not only did it comprise some of the best sugar plantations in Upper Egypt, but its infrastructure was second to none. It included 470 kilometres of railroads, 65 locomotives and 2,092 wagons, nine sugar mills, substantial irrigation and drainage canals, Nile steamers, tugs and barges, warehouses, crops in the fields, cattle and even entire towns.

Conventional wisdom insisted that with sound administration, a privatized Daira Sanieh could become the inspiration for and engine of a rejuvenated economy.

And so it was that the landmark sale of the Daira Sanieh transferred 100 percent of the agricultural conglomerate to the private sector and was instrumental in the founding of the National Bank of Egypt. Furthermore it helped create a new-rich class of local landed gentry thus sparking an unprecedented era of economic well-being. Not bad for a single anchor-investor deal!

The timeline of the Daira's sale was as follows:

On 21 June 1898, an arrangement was reached whereby the government sold the Daira estates to an international consortium led by London's Sir Ernest Cassel for the sum of £6,431,500 sterling, representing the Daira's outstanding liabilities. This singular transfer of ownership and control from a state-owned enterprise to the private sector would change the economic and social face of Egypt for at least the next 60 years.

Four days later, three out of the four new owners of the Daira Sanieh created the National Bank of Egypt, which henceforth served as the country's regulatory and issue bank until 1960. The four new owners of the Daira Sanieh were: Ernest Cassel 50%, Ernest Cronier 12.5%, Raphael Suarès 25%, and M. Cattaui 12.5%.

These two developments — the privatization of the Daira Sanieh and the creation of the bank — were part of a plan conceived in part by Egypt's de facto ruler, Sir Evelyn Baring (later Lord Cromer, the British proconsul in Egypt) along with Cassel and his powerful banking allies.

With the Daira lands in hand, the consortium proceeded to develop the first generation of modern agro-industrial

General Debt of the Daira Sanieh

Bonds of the "General Debt of the Daira Sanieh" were devised by the Egyptian Government by Khedive Tewfik's two decrees dated June 6 and July 5 1890. The proceedings were to be applied to the redemption of the Unified Debt by the "Caisse de la Dette Publique", an international financial commission entrusted with the task of regulating Egypts' debts to European countries. Transactions pertaining to this 4% Bond-to-Bearer were implemented through:
Paris: Banque de Paris et de Pay Bas.
London: Messrs Stern Brothers.
Berlin: Messrs Robert Warschauer & Co.
Frankfort-on-Maine: Messrs Jacob S. H. Stern.
Egypt: Suarès Frères & Co.

GOUVERNEMENT ÉGYPTIEN

Dette générale de la Daïra Sanieh

4 %

Créée en vertu des Décrets de S. A. le Khédive, en date des 6 Juin et 5 Juillet 1890

DONT LE TEXTE EST REPRODUIT CI-CONTRE

MONTANT DE LA DETTE :

£ 7,299,360 ou Fr. 182,484,000

DIVISÉ EN TITRES

de £ 20 ou Fr. 500, de £ 100 ou Fr. 2,500
de £ 500 ou Fr. 12,500, de £ 1,000 ou Fr. 25,000

Le Gouvernement Égyptien s'engage à ne pas rembourser la Dette générale de la Daïra Sanieh avant le 15 Octobre 1905, sauf l'amortissement prévu aux articles 7 et 8 du décret du 6 Juin 1890.

Sont maintenues au profit des titres de la présente Émission toutes les dispositions relatives à l'administration, aux garanties et aux affectations hypothécaires assurées aux Obligations de la Dette générale de la Daïra Sanieh. *(Art. 2.- Décret du 6 Juin 1890.)*

Obligation au Porteur

DE FR. 500

EGYPTIAN GOVERNMENT

General Debt of the Daïra Sanieh

4 %

Created in virtue of the Decrees of H. H. the Khedive dated 6th June and 5th July 1890

THE TEXT OF WHICH IS PRINTED ON THE REVERSE

AMOUNT OF STOCK :

£ 7,299,360 or Fr. 182,484,000

DIVIDED IN BONDS

of £ 20 or Fr. 500, of £ 100 or Fr. 2,500
of £ 500 or Fr. 12,500, of £ 1,000 or Fr. 25,000

The Egyptian Government undertakes not to reimburse the General Debt of the Daïra Sanieh before the 15th October 1905, except the amortization stipulated in articles 7 and 8 of the decree of 6th June 1890.

All the dispositions regarding the administration, the guarantees and the mortgage assured to the General Debt of the Daïra Sanieh, are maintained in favour of the new Loan. *(Art. 2. — Decree of 6th June 1890.)*

Bond to Bearer

FOR £ 20

Nº

INTÉRÊT ANNUEL : FR. 20 OU £ 0:16.0

Payable par semestre, les 15 Avril et 15 Octobre

au CAIRE, à PARIS, à LONDRES, à BERLIN et à FRANCFORT s/M.

Le paiement des coupons semestriels et le remboursement des Obligations seront, **en tout temps, affranchis de tout impôt ou taxe,** de quelque nature que ce soit, au profit du Gouvernement Égyptien.

Pour Contrôle :

ANNUAL INTEREST : £ 0:16.0 OR FR. 20

Payable half-yearly on the 15th of April and the 15th of October

in CAIRO, PARIS, LONDON, BERLIN and FRANKFORT o/M.

The payment of the half-yearly coupons and the reimbursement of the Bonds **are for ever free of tax** whatever benefiting the Egyptian Government.

Au nom du Conseil de Direction de la Daïra Sanieh :

Les Obligations de la Dette générale de la Daïra Sanieh 4 % sont divisées comme suit :

131,468	Titres de Fr.	500	Nos 000,001 à 131,468.	Fr. 65,734,000
23,280	—	2,500	— 131,469 à 154,748.	— 58,200,000
3,264	—	12,500	— 154,749 à 158,012.	— 40,800,000
710	—	25,000	— 158,013 à 158,722.	— 17,750,000
158,722	Titres			Fr. 182,484,000

The Bonds of the General Debt of the Daïra Sanieh 4 % are divided as follows:

131,468	Bonds of £	20	Nos 000,001 to 131,468.	£ 2,629,360
23,280	—	100	— 131,469 to 154,748.	— 2,328,000
3,264	—	500	— 154,749 to 158,012.	— 1,632,000
710	—	1,000	— 158,013 to 158,722.	— 710,000
158,722	Bonds			£ 7,299,360

IMPRIMERIE CHAIX, 20, RUE BERGÈRE, PARIS. — 16727-7-90.

concerns in Egypt. By the same token, privatizing the Daira Sanieh spawned the mammoth projects of two Nile reservoirs at Aswan and Qena.

Naturally, these projects created massive numbers of jobs and lucrative export markets. Aside from multiplying the agricultural land acreage and establishing Egypt's first system of perennial irrigation, the two reservoirs also provided cheap electricity, a new commodity for which demand was rapidly rising.

As an overall result, the value of the consortium's land rose so sharply that when the group sold the Daira's agricultural properties on the open market, the revenues exceeded the outstanding portion of the consortium's loan, leaving a huge profit on the transaction. To this end, the company split with the government so that the latter could finally liquidate the debt for which the Daira Sanieh had been held collateral.

Meanwhile, the consortium continued to strip the Daira's assets by selling off its sugar mills, railways and rolling stock to the newly incorporated sugar refinery, which immediately became Egypt's largest industrial concern.

It was the sale between 1900 and 1906 of the Daira's remaining land amounting to approximately 300,000 feddans that spawned the first generation of large landowners and entrepreneurs from outside the foreign and Turco-Circassian classes. The omdas, sheikhs al-balad and effendis who became wealthy landowners, entrepreneurs and brokers were branded the nouveau riche of their time, and were the forerunners of Egypt's intelligentsia, politicians and civil servants.

Then as now, privatization was not without its opponents, especially those in patronage posts, living comfortably under the old quasi-public regime. And even though some of their cries of foul play were justified, capitalism had won the day. The country had set off full throttle toward a modern era. New capital markets were about to be created and Egypt's nominal age of enlightenment, secularization and opportunity was about to begin. Few suspected that a century later Egypt would find itself on the same threshold of change.

It is noteworthy to mention here that from among the first members of the board of the newly privatized Daira Sanieh only one was Egyptian; the rest of the directors, known as Cassel's men, were either Europeans or Jews: Sir Vincent Caillard, Sir William Ward, Sir Edward Elias Sasson, Earl (H.J.) Cairns, Carl Meyer, R. Miller; Sir Elwin Palmer, Raphael Suarès, Simon Rolo, Ali Sharaawi Bey, Philippe Borelli Bey, F. Dusseigneur and William Willcocks.

Notwithstanding the sterling reputation and business acumen of these gentlemen, the privatization of Daira Sanieh and its lucrative results was the result of Sir Ernest Cassel's farsightedness. So successful were his schemes in Egypt that the amount loaned out for the construction of the Aswan Reservoir was fully repaid by 1914. Likewise, his investments in the Daira Sanieh were equally profitable with the Daira loan being repaid in full very shortly after its privatization.

National Bank of Egypt

Established by the Khedivial Decree of June 25, 1898 with the exclusive right to issue notes payable at sight to Bearer. An agreement was reached in 1940 between the Egyptian Governemnt and the Natioanl Bank of Egypt regarding the renewal of the bank's charter which would normally have expired on June 25, 1948. The new charter was for forty years effective August 12, 1940.

Head Office: 24 Kasr el-Nil Street, Cairo.

Capital:
Paid-Up Capital £3,000,000
Reserve Funds £3,000,000
£3,000,000 divided in 300,000 Ordinary shares of £10 each, fully paid.

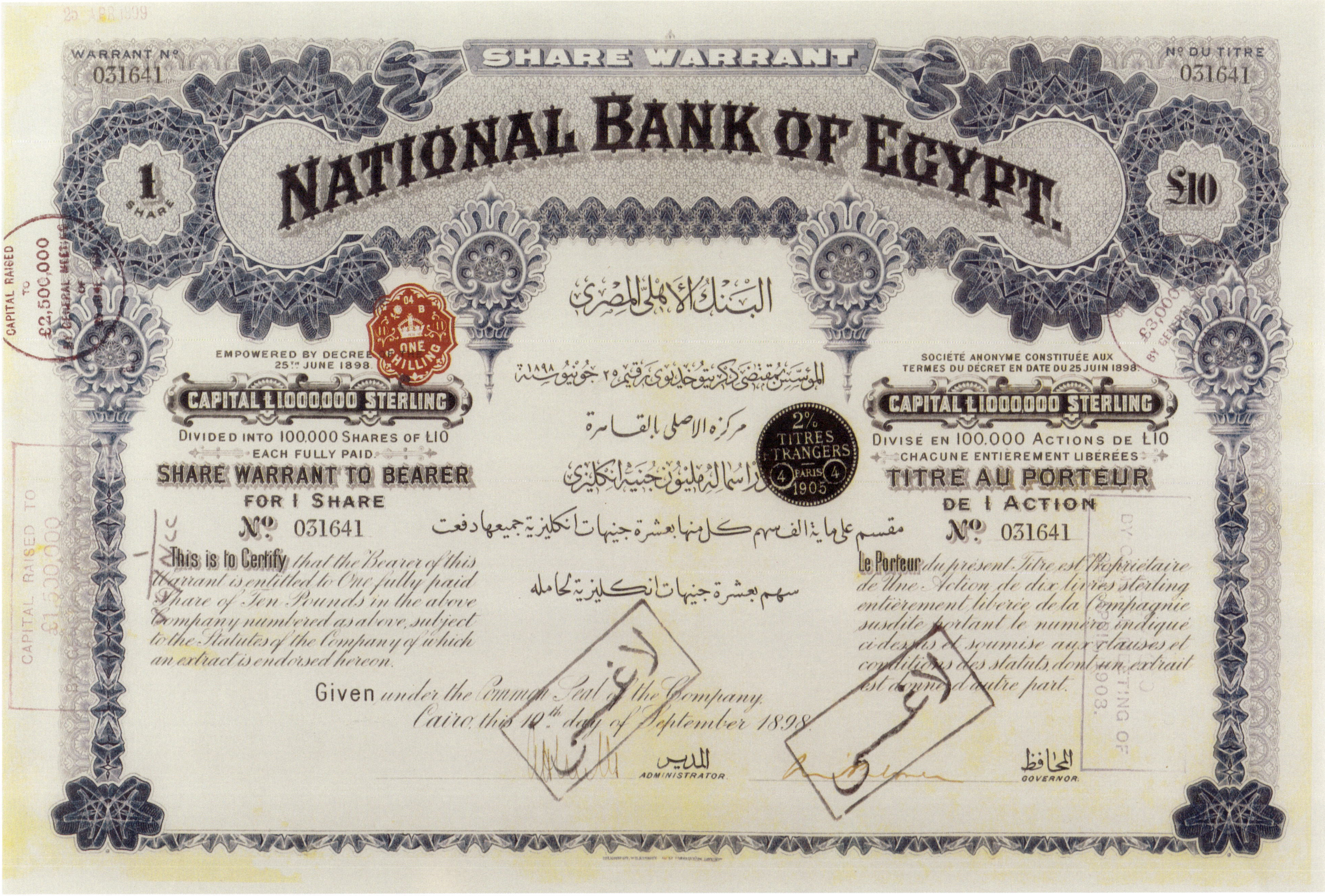

WARRANT Nº 031641

SHARE WARRANT

Nº DU TITRE 031641

NATIONAL BANK OF EGYPT.

1 SHARE

£10

البنك الأهلي المصري

EMPOWERED BY DECREE 25TH JUNE 1898.

الموسس بمقتضى دكريتو خديوى رقيم ٢٥ جونيو سنة ١٨٩٨

SOCIÉTÉ ANONYME CONSTITUÉE AUX TERMES DU DÉCRET EN DATE DU 25 JUIN 1898.

CAPITAL £1,000,000 STERLING

مركزه الاصلى بالقاهرة

CAPITAL £1,000,000 STERLING

DIVIDED INTO 100,000 SHARES OF £10 EACH FULLY PAID

راسماله مليون جنيه انكليزى

DIVISÉ EN 100,000 ACTIONS DE £10 CHACUNE ENTIÈREMENT LIBÉRÉES

SHARE WARRANT TO BEARER FOR 1 SHARE

TITRE AU PORTEUR DE 1 ACTION

Nº 031641

مقسم على ماية الف سهم كل منها بعشرة جنيهات انكليزية جميعها دفعت

Nº 031641

This is to Certify *that the Bearer of this Warrant is entitled to One fully paid Share of Ten Pounds in the above Company numbered as above, subject to the Statutes of the Company of which an extract is endorsed hereon.*

سهم بعشرة جنيهات انكليزية لحامله

Le Porteur *du présent Titre est Propriétaire de Une Action de dix livres sterling entièrement libérée de la Compagnie susdite portant le numéro indiqué ci-dessus et soumise aux clauses et conditions des statuts dont un extrait est donné d'autre part.*

Given *under the Common Seal of the Company. Cairo, this 10th day of September 1898.*

المدير
ADMINISTRATOR

المحافظ
GOVERNOR

ONE SHILLING

2% TITRES ÉTRANGERS PARIS 1905

CAPITAL RAISED TO £2,500,000 BY GENERAL MEETING

CAPITAL RAISED TO £1,500,000

£3,000,000 BY GENERAL MEETING OF ... 1903.

Sir Ernest Joseph Cassel and the National Bank of Egypt

From his Park Lane office in London, Cassel led the tiny group that created Egypt's embryonic central bank. While Cassel represented British interests, it was for the Suarès Brothers of Cairo and Constantine Salvagos of Alexandria to represent local capital.

Capitalized at one million pounds, the colonial bank's main purpose was to provide the means of channeling finance to development projects and to attract British capital and enterprise. What made this bank different was its charter which gave it, with Whitehall's blessings no doubt, exclusive right to issue notes, a privilege which it started to exercise as of 3 April 1899.

Despite his initial 50% equity share, Cassel never actually attended to running the bank. For that, he was represented over two decades on the board by three important bankers.

Sir Vincent Caillard (1856-1930) was a director of several Cassel-owned companies including Vickers Sons.

Sir Sydney Cornwalis Peel (1870-1938) was Cassel's right arm in all Egyptian capital ventures. A son of Viscount Peel, Sir Sydney was also the first chairman of the Agriculture Bank of Egypt.

Carl Meyer (1851-1922) was the Hamburg-born private secretary of Alfred de Rothschild and later the chairman of the National Bank of Egypt's London committee. On the board of a number of blue chip financial houses, Meyer was also vice-chairman of De Beers Consolidated and a director of the Hong Kong & Shanghai Bank. He would receive a peerage (Lord Shortgrove) in 1910.

The bank's first governor was Sir Elwin Palmer. Although indebted to Cassel, he was regarded more as a Cromer man, reporting directly to the British proconsul, which often led to dicey situations. Cassel and Cromer did not always see eye to eye. They both claimed long connections to Egypt, Cromer since his appointment to the Caisse de la Dette and Cassel since the days when he apprenticed at the Anglo-Egyptian Bank in Paris.

With so many investments along the Nile valley, it was not surprising that Egypt would become Cassel's favorite winter resort traveling there each year accompanied by his wife and daughter, or alternately with his lifelong friend, the American railway baron, Jacob Henry Schiff.

From Sir Elwin Palmer in 1898 down to Sir Edward Cook in 1940, the National Bank's chief executive was always British which led critics to observe that not only was it a colonial bank, but its membership was closed to all but the cream of the English rank and file in Egypt. In a sense, they were not far off. This was no rags to riches bank that grew because of ordinary depositors' savings. This was a trailblazing institution which, from its outset, was meant to serve British trade and colonial interests.

Cassel enjoyed better relations with the proconsul's brother, Edward Charles Baring (Lord Revelstoke). It helped that Lord Revelstoke was also a senior partner in Baring Brothers and a director of the Bank of England. It was

Building Lands of Egypt

Registered on May 30, 1905 to carry out general land business. The company went into voluntary liquidation on December 31, 1918. The remaining assets in December 1950 consisted of land in Victoria and Abu Nawatir in Ramleh, Alexandria.

Office: 3 Mohamed Aly Square, Alexandria

Capital:
L.E. 312,000 in 80,000 £4 shares.
2,000 Founders shares of no nominal value.

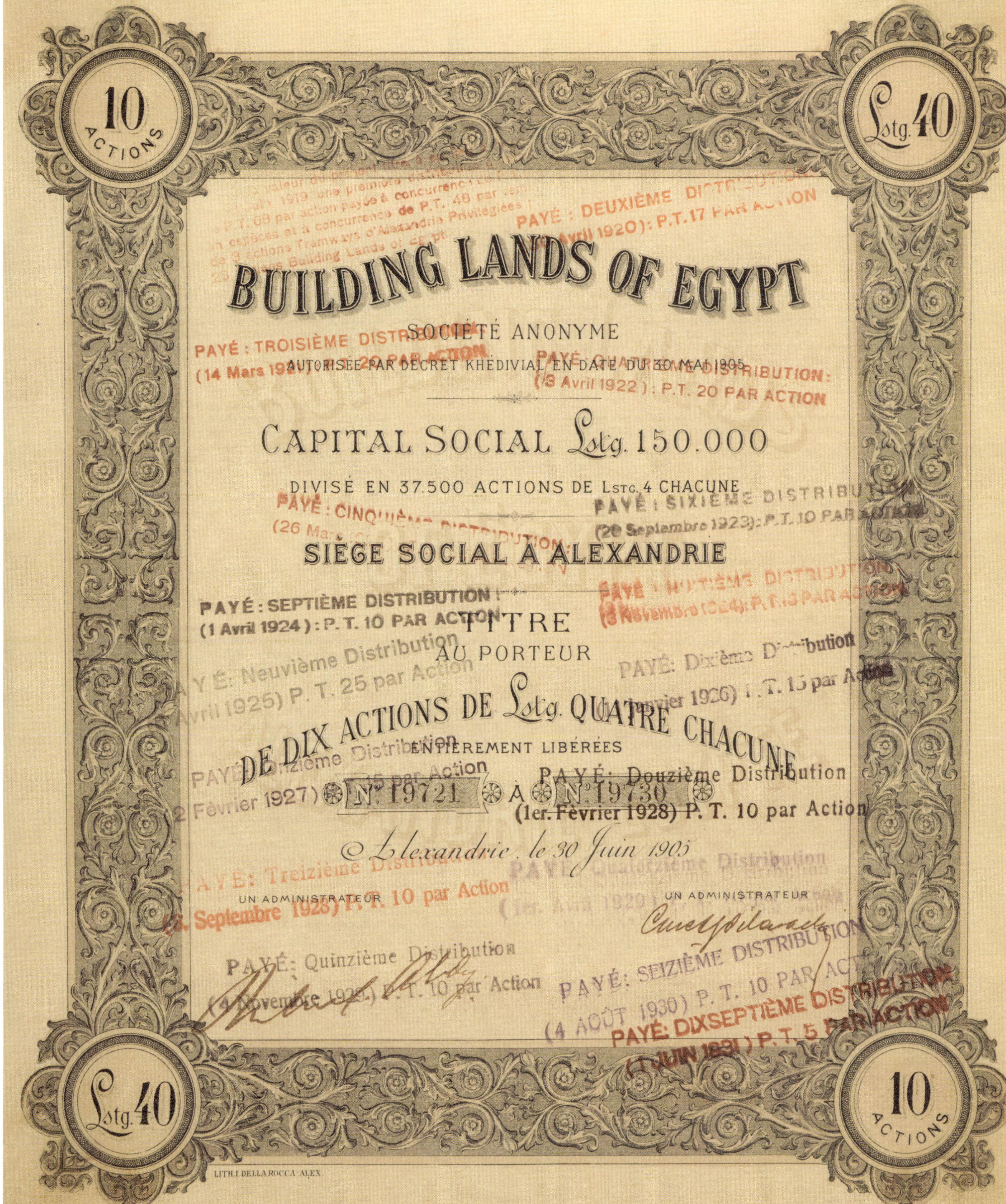
10 ACTIONS

Lstg. 40

BUILDING LANDS OF EGYPT

SOCIÉTÉ ANONYME

AUTORISÉE PAR DÉCRET KHÉDIVIAL EN DATE DU 30 MAI 1905

CAPITAL SOCIAL Lstg. 150.000

DIVISÉ EN 37.500 ACTIONS DE Lstg. 4 CHACUNE

SIÈGE SOCIAL À ALEXANDRIE

TITRE AU PORTEUR

DE DIX ACTIONS DE Lstg. QUATRE CHACUNE

ENTIÈREMENT LIBÉRÉES

Nº 19721 À Nº 19730

Alexandrie, le 30 Juin 1905

UN ADMINISTRATEUR

UN ADMINISTRATEUR

PAYÉ : DEUXIÈME DISTRIBUTION (... Avril 1920) : P.T. 17 PAR ACTION

PAYÉ : TROISIÈME DISTRIBUTION (14 Mars 1921) : P.T. 20 PAR ACTION

PAYÉ : QUATRIÈME DISTRIBUTION : (3 Avril 1922) : P.T. 20 PAR ACTION

PAYÉ : CINQUIÈME DISTRIBUTION (26 Mars ...)

PAYÉ : SIXIÈME DISTRIBUTION (20 Septembre 1923) : P.T. 10 PAR ACTION

PAYÉ : SEPTIÈME DISTRIBUTION : (1 Avril 1924) : P.T. 10 PAR ACTION

PAYÉ : HUITIÈME DISTRIBUTION (3 Novembre 1924) : P.T. 15 PAR ACTION

PAYÉ : Neuvième Distribution (... Avril 1925) P. T. 25 par Action

PAYÉ : Dixième Distribution (... Janvier 1926) P. T. 15 par Action

PAYÉ : Onzième Distribution (2 Février 1927) P. T. 15 par Action

PAYÉ : Douzième Distribution (1er. Février 1928) P. T. 10 par Action

PAYÉ : Treizième Distribution (3 Septembre 1928) P. T. 10 par Action

PAYÉ : Quatorzième Distribution (1er. Avril 1929) P. T. 10 par Action

PAYÉ : Quinzième Distribution (4 Novembre 1929) P. T. 10 par Action

PAYÉ : SEIZIÈME DISTRIBUTION (4 AOÛT 1930) P. T. 10 PAR ACTION

PAYÉ : DIXSEPTIÈME DISTRIBUTION (1 JUIN 1931) P. T. 5 PAR ACTION

LITH. I. DELLA ROCCA - ALEX.

at the Baring's famous country seat, Nubia House, that Cassel concluded several lucrative Egyptian deals. To Lord Cromer's annoyance, Cassel also enjoyed cordial relations with Egypt's Khedive. In June 1903, Cassel was instrumental in setting up a meeting in England between the Khedive and King Edward VII. While in London, the Khedive was Cassel's guest at his No. 48 Grosvenor Square mansion.

In 1904, Cassel loaned Khedive Abbas Hilmi 500,000 pounds at the low rate of 2.5% in return for new land and commercial concessions in Upper Egypt. This direct way of doing business with the Khedive without first consulting with the British Residency in Cairo greatly irritated Cromer. To mollify the rancorous British proconsul, Cassel donated 41,000 pounds towards the establishment of the Traveling Eye (trachoma) Clinic in Egypt and gave an equally generous sum for the creation of the Anglo-American Hospital in Cairo. In 1912, five years after Cromer retired from Egypt, Cassel gave the sum of 10,000 pounds to the Deaconess's Hospital in Alexandria.

Confidante to the British monarch and adviser to the Egyptian khedive, Cassel was rewarded for his efforts when, in 1902, he was made a member of King Edward's Privy Council. Several months later, he received the Grand Cordon of the Imperial Ottoman Order of the Osmanieh from a grateful Khedive.

Sir Ernest Cassel died in 1921. The following year, his granddaughter Edwina would marry a senior member of European royalty eventually becoming the Vicereine of India as Lady Mountbatten.

Commercial Bank of Egypt

Established on November 10, 1920 with branches in London, Paris and New York.

Alexandria Office: 11 Avenue Fouad I.
Cairo Branch: 33 Soliman Pasha Street.

Capital:
£1,200,000 divided into 300,000 Ordinary shares of £4 each, fully paid.

Commercial Bank of Egypt

Banque Commerciale d'Egypte

SOCIÉTÉ ANONYME ÉGYPTIENNE

Créée par Décret Sultanien en date du 10 Novembre 1920

CAPITAL AUTORISÉ
Lstg. 1,200,000

CAPITAL VERSÉ
Lstg. 1,200,000

REPRÉSENTÉ PAR
300.000 ACTIONS DE Lstg. 4. CHACUNE
entièrement libérées

(Décisions des Assemblées Générales Extraordinaires des 3 et 31 Janvier 1946)

TITRE AU PORTEUR
DE
Vingt Cinq Actions de Lstg. 4 CHACUNE

Le Porteur du présent titre est propriétaire de Vingt Cinq Actions de Quatre Lstg. chacune entièrement libérées de la Société susdite, portant les N.os ci-dessous et soumises aux clauses et conditions des Statuts.

البنك التجاري المصري
شركة مساهمة مصرية
مؤسسة بمرسوم سلطاني صادر بتاريخ ١٠ نوفمبر ١٩٢٠
رأس المال المصرح به ١٢٠٠٠٠٠ جنيه انجليزي
رأس المال المدفوع ١٢٠٠٠٠٠ جنيه انجليزي
مؤلف من
٣٠٠٠٠٠ سهم قيمة كل سهم
اربعة جنيهات انجليزية مدفوعة كلها
بقرار الجمعية العمومية الغير عادية
بجلستيها في ٣ و ٣١ يناير ١٩٤٦
سند لحامله
عن خمسة وعشرين سهما قيمة السهم الواحد
اربعة جنيهات انجليزية
حامل هذا السند يمتلك خمسة وعشرين سهما
قيمتها مائة جنيه انجليزي مدفوعة بكاملها من أسهم
الشركة المذكورة تحت النمر الموضحة أدناه

Commercial Bank of Egypt

S.A.E.

Created by Sultanian Decree of the 10th November 1920

AUTHORISED CAPITAL
Lstg. 1,200,000

CAPITAL PAID UP
Lstg. 1,200,000

REPRESENTED BY
300.000 SHARES OF Lstg. 4. EACH
fully paid

(Decisions of the Extraordinary General Meetings of the 3 and 31 January 1946)

SHARE WARRANT TO BEARER
FOR
Twenty Five Shares of Lstg. 4 EACH

This is to certify that the bearer of this Warrant is entitled to Twenty Five fully paid shares of Four Pounds Sterling each, in the above Company numbered as below subject to the Statutes of the Company.

TITRE AYANT PARTICIPÉ À LA RÉDUCTION DE CAPITAL SUIVANT DÉCISIONS DES ASSEMBLÉES GÉNÉRALES EXTRAORDINAIRES DES 28 AVRIL ET 27 MAI 1950

VINGT CINQ ACTIONS N.o A 187526 à N.o A 187550

DÉLIVRÉES SOUS LE SCEAU DE LA BANQUE À ALEXANDRIE

UN ADMINISTRATEUR: L'ADMINISTRATEUR-DÉLÉGUÉ:

COMMERCIAL BANK OF EGYPT — SOCIÉTÉ ANONYME ÉGYPTIENNE

LITH. F.lli VENTURA ALEXANDRIE

Commercial Bank of Egypt — SOCIÉTÉ ANONYME ÉGYPTIENNE — VINGT CINQ ACTIONS AU PORTEUR — N.o A187526 à N.o A187550 — COUPON N.o 24

Commercial Bank of Egypt — SOCIÉTÉ ANONYME ÉGYPTIENNE — VINGT CINQ ACTIONS AU PORTEUR — N.o A187526 à N.o A187550 — COUPON N.o 23

Commercial Bank of Egypt — SOCIÉTÉ ANONYME ÉGYPTIENNE — VINGT CINQ ACTIONS AU PORTEUR — N.o A187526 à N.o A187550 — COUPON N.o 22

Commercial Bank of Egypt — SOCIÉTÉ ANONYME ÉGYPTIENNE — VINGT CINQ ACTIONS AU PORTEUR — N.o A187526 à N.o A187550 — COUPON N.o 21

The Suarès Bothers of Cairo

With the blessings of Whitehall in London and Lord Cromer in Cairo, Sir Ernest Cassel put up 50% of the National Bank of Egypt's founding capital ensuring Britain a lion's share of all new major capital investments in Egypt.

Britain meanwhile actively pursued a stringent policy of fiscal reforms in Egypt aimed at enhancing investments in land, irrigation and transport, with the hope of setting off a splurge of capital accumulation. Because the National Bank was a pivotal component of these reforms, it was of paramount importance to legitimize its position as an "Egyptian" bank by recruiting local partners. Raphael Isaac Suarès was one of the two "Egyptian" partners who would found the National Bank of Egypt.

Apart from the Khedivial family and its immediate circle, it was the thriving Ottoman-Levantine elite which dominated Cairo and Alexandria's commercial and banking scene. Being a leading member of this distinguished elite, Suarès also enjoyed a measure of political power due to his diligent cultivation of the representatives of the European powers in Egypt. Moreover, he was affiliated with the Khedivial family through his step daughter, Alix Marthe Frezet, who had married the Khedive's cousin, Prince Ali Fazil.

Through his bank, Suarès Freres & Cie., Raphael Suarès subscribed to 25% of National Bank of Egypt's founding shares. In an effort to spread his risks, he brought in his brothers, Joseph and Felix, as well as the owners of several Jewish banking houses to whom he was related by marriage. The most renowned amongst them being: J.N. Mosseri Figli & Co., Yacoub Moise Cattaui Fils & Cie., J. Levi Menashe Fils & Cie. and R. Rolo Figli & Co.

A large majority of these *mutamessereen* or pseudo-Egyptians came to Egypt during Mohammed Ali's boom years. While many came from within the Ottoman Empire (Salonika, Smyrna, Aleppo, Constantinople, Baghdad), there were those like Suarès who had come from the southern European port cities of Trieste and Leghorn. Only the Cattauis from the above assembly claimed long ancestry in Egypt. Not surprisingly, there was a perception among the local population that minority groups dominated intermediary economic positions. This earned them some degree of envy and hostility. But in fact, the true culprit was the system of Capitulations from which the Suarès and their associates benefited.

Capitulations in the Ottoman Empire were not unlike the unpopular Concession system in Shanghai. In Egypt, alien (and sometimes local) minorities having grasped the advantages of such a system, quickly placed themselves under the protection of a European power. This allowed them to reap economic benefits while maintaining a status of extra-territoriality exempting them from local taxes and local jurisprudence. Armed with this protection, the Suarès and their kith joined the board of the National Bank of Egypt. From a European investor's point of view, Raphael Suarès and his associates, while not bona fide Egyptians, were perceived as the ideal capitalist go-between who could merge Egypt's surplus resources with foreign venture capital. That they had already culturally gravitated towards France and England made them even more appealing.

Egyptian Delta Light Railways

Registered in England on March 4, 1897 with the object of acquiring the shares of La Societe Egyptienne des Chemins de Fer Agricole and the Compagnie des Chemins de Fer Economiques de l'Est Egyptien. The former held a concession from the Egyptian Governemnt for the construction of light lines in the provinces of Behera and Gharbieh and the latter a similar concession in Charkieh, Dakahlieh and Kalioubieh. Over and above, Delta Light Railways' concession includes a monopoly for light railways of 75 centimetres (2 feet 5 ½ inches) for an intermediate period. An aggregate of 977 kilometres were open and working on March 31, 1946.

Cairo Office: 40 Giza Road, Giza, Cairo.

Capital:
£1,040,599 in 104,078 dividend shares each yielding 5½%. Cumulative Preference shares of £10 each, fully paid, issued at different rates.
£110,000 divided into 11,000 Deferred shares of £10 each, fully paid.

Nº 1456

THE EGYPTIAN DELTA
LIGHT RAILWAYS' LTD.
£100
COUPONS ... OF
COUPONS Nos 100 TO 109
ISSUED

THE EGYPTIAN DELTA LIGHT RAILWAYS, LIMITED.

25 TEN SHILLINGS 97 10

CAPITAL £280,000.

In 28,000 Shares divided into 21,000 5½ per cent. Preference Shares of £10 each and 7,000 Deferred Shares of £10 each.

Issue of Debentures for £170,000, in 1,700 Debentures of £100 each payable to Bearer, Nos. 1 to 1,700 both inclusive, bearing interest at the rate of £4 per cent. per annum, repayable at par on the 1st day of April, 1947, with power:—

(a) To purchase the Debentures at 103 per cent. at any time after the expiration of 25 years on giving six months' notice,
(b) To purchase Debentures in the market at any time for cancellation, and
(c) To issue Debentures or Debenture Stock ranking *pari passu* with the present Issue, provided that the total amount of the Debentures or Debenture Stock of the Company issued as part of the first charge shall not exceed the amount of the Preference Capital of the Company for the time being subscribed.

Issued under the authority of Article 16 of the Articles of Association of the Company and in pursuance of a Resolution of the Board of Directors of the 25th March, 1897.

DEBENTURE.

This Debenture is now irredeemable and carries interest at the rate of 5 per cent. per annum. (see Indorsement.)

In consideration of the sum of £100 paid to The Egyptian Delta Light Railways, Limited (hereinafter referred to as "the Company"), the Company will on the 1st day of April, 1947, pay the original holder or other the bearer hereof the sum of £100.

And the Company will in the meantime pay interest on the said sum of £100 at the rate of £4 per cent. per annum, the first payment of such interest to be for six months (less five days) and to be payable on the 1st day of April, 1898, subsequent interest to be paid by equal half-yearly payments on the 1st day of April and the 1st day of October in each year, all in accordance with the coupons annexed hereto. And the said Company doth hereby as security for the payment of the said capital moneys and interest charge (as a first charge having priority over all other charges created or to be created by the Company) all its property, undertaking and assets both present and future including its unpaid calls and uncalled capital for the time being.

Provided always that until the principal monies hereby secured shall become payable in accordance with the Conditions endorsed hereon, this Debenture shall except as in the Deed hereinafter mentioned or in the Conditions endorsed hereon, be a floating charge only and shall not interfere with the receipt or payment of any moneys arising from Calls or otherwise or the payment of dividends, but shall in like manner attach to the proceeds of any sale, dealing or other disposition, and any property and moneys for the time being acquired or held by the Company, provided that the Company shall not have power to create any charge in priority to the charge hereby made.

This Debenture is issued upon and subject to the conditions endorsed hereon, which shall be deemed to be incorporated herewith, and to the provisions of the Deed referred to in such Conditions (including provisions whereby a majority of the Debenture Holders in meeting may bind a minority).

This Debenture is one of a series secured by an Indenture dated the 25th day of March, 1897, made between the Company of the one part, and the Right Hon. William Lidderdale and Sir Gerald Fitzgerald, K.C.M.G. (therein called the Trustees) of the other part, and is issued upon and subject to the above conditions which are deemed to be incorporated with the said Debentures and to the provisions of the said Deed.

Given under the Common Seal of the Company this 5th day of October, 1897.

Robt Miller Director.

E. Mein Secretary.

A. P. Blundell, Taylor & Co., Printers, 173, Upper Thames Street, E.C. Telephone No. 936 (Bank)

The mercantile father, Isaac Suarès, spared nothing towards educating his sons: Felix, Joseph and Raphael. The financial payoff was astounding for both the Suarès dynasty and for their country of adoption.

In 1880, the Suarès name had already made headlines when, with French partners, the Suarès family helped create the Credit Foncier Egyptien. Despite a bumpy start, this monumental commercial undertaking ultimately did away with money-grabbing usurers while laying the seeds for agricultural reforms.

The Suarès name was equally celebrated in the field of transport when Isaac launched Cairo's first modern public transport service dubbed *arabiyaat Sawarez*, where a pay-as-you-ride horse-drawn omnibus plied defined urban routes, one of them going as far as Bassatine, east of Cairo.

Another transport milestone occurred in 1889 when Isaac's sons launched Egypt's first suburban railway, running from Bab al-Louk to Helwan. Other important Suarès-controlled railways included the Egyptian Delta Light Railway in Lower Egypt and the Qena-Aswan Railway in the South.

Raising the required capital for land purchases, rolling stock and chain gangs, was no problem. The Suarèses either owned or were connected with Egypt's principal investment houses earning them the sobriquet of Egypt's Rothschilds. And like the original Rothschilds, they too had become lenders to the Khedive which in those days meant the State.

The Suarès holdings were greatly enhanced when Suarès partnered with Sir Ernest Cassel to purchase from the Egyptian government the former Khedivial estates of Daira Sanieh.

The lucrative association with Cassel notwithstanding, it was through his French associates that Suarès participated in the epic undertaking of overhauling part of Egypt's agricultural sector. Together, they purchased and modernized Mohammed Ali's antiquated sugar mills adding new refineries up and down the Nile, including a large one in Hawamdia.

When it came to real estate development, the Suarès brothers were responsible for much of Helwan's modern utilities and pleasure institutions. Not only did they control the spa's thermal baths, hotels and casinos, but it was Felix Suarès who turned on the town's first electric street lamps in a much publicized event in 1899.

Continuing to capitalize on the economic boom brought on by privatization, Felix and his relations concluded in 1904 a deal calling for the creation of a well-conceived garden suburb midway along their suburban railway line. They would call their new development Maadi.

Recognition by the State and its rulers — British and Egyptian alike — was never far behind. Summarizing it best are the words bestowed by Khedive Abbas Hilmi II on his financial advisor Raphael Suarès on the occasion of the February 1909 re-launch of the Naga Hamadi sugar refinery.

In the presence of his royal guest and the other members of the sugar company's board, Suarès, as principal

Societé Generale des Sucreries et de la Raffinerie d'Égypte

Established by the merger in April 26, 1897 of the Sucreries de la Haute-Egypte (registered on April 12, 1892), and the Sucrerie-Raffinerie d'Egypte (registered on July 13, 1893).

The Company owns sugar-mills in Upper Egypt at Sheikh Fadl, Abou Gourgas, Nag Hamadi, Ermant, and Kom Ombo, and a refinery at Hawamdieh. The Hawamdieh refinery, 28 kilometres south of Cairo, is the third largest in the world. It has an average daily production of about 700,000 kg of refined sugar, with a possible output capacity of 1,000,000 kg a day. Its extensive buildings cover more than 40 feddans. The company employs at the sugar-mills and the refinery an estimated 27,000 workers. The sugar industry in Egypt, which operates under a protective tariff is controlled by the Societe Generale des Sucreries et de la Raffinerie d'Egypte. All the cane required for its mills is obtained locally.

Sugar-cane cultivation was introduced in Egypt around 1850. Certain species of cane were brought from the East Indies for plantation on lands belonging to the Daira Sanieh in Upper Egypt. Sugar extraction did not begin until 1855 at the Rodah factory of the Daira Sanieh. By 1870, there were 17 factories for raw sugar, which until 1881 was sent to Marseille for refining.

Head Office: 12 Talaat Harb Pasha Street (ex. Aboul Sebaa), Cairo.

Capital:
L.E. 923,636 divided in 239,439 Preference shares of FF 100 each, fully paid, redeemable at FF 125 only in the event of a winding up.
L.E. 417,898 in 108,334 Ordinary shares of FF 100 each, fully paid.
38,600 Founders shares of no par value.

Société Générale

des Sucreries et de la Raffinerie d'Égypte

SOCIÉTÉ ANONYME ÉGYPTIENNE

Autorisée par Firman Khédivial du 12 Avril 1892.

Capital social : TRENTE-QUATRE MILLIONS HUIT CENT QUATRE-VINGT-CINQ MILLE SEPT CENTS Francs

DIVISÉ EN 348.857 ACTIONS DE 100 FRANCS CHACUNE, ENTIÈREMENT LIBÉRÉES, DONT :

240.523 ACTIONS PRIVILÉGIÉES, REMBOURSABLES A 125 FR. (24.052.300 FR.), 108.334 ACTIONS ORDINAIRES, REMBOURSABLES A 100 FR. (10.833.400 FR.)

Ainsi établi par décision de l'Assemblée générale du 24 Mars 1906 et en suite du Concordat homologué par jugement du Tribunal mixte du Caire, le 2 Juin 1906.

SIÈGE SOCIAL AU CAIRE

ÉMISSION DE 109.000 OBLIGATIONS

De 400 Francs chacune.

Ces Obligations ont été créées en règlement de créances antérieures, aux termes du Concordat voté au Caire le 23 Mai 1906 et homologué par jugement du Tribunal mixte du Caire le 2 Juin 1906.

VI
1 1 V

Obligation 5 % de Quatre Cents Francs au Porteur

N° 051,520

à revenu variable

PAYABLE PAR SEMESTRE, A PARIS ET AU CAIRE, A PARTIR DU 1er JUILLET 1909, DANS LES TERMES DU CONCORDAT DU 23 MAI 1906

Titre remboursable à 500 francs, au plus tard en soixante ans, à partir du 31 Décembre 1909, par voie de tirages au sort semestriels qui auront lieu les 1er Avril et 1er Octobre de chaque année, et pouvant être racheté en Bourse s'il est coté au-dessous de 500 francs. L'intérêt attaché au Titre cessera à partir du jour fixé pour le remboursement.

La propriété de ce Titre emportera de plein droit adhésion au « Syndicat des porteurs d'obligations à revenu variable de la Société des Sucreries et de la Raffinerie d'Egypte », formé suivant acte sous seings privés déposé chez Me ARON, Notaire à Paris, le 31 Janvier 1906.

Les Titres et les Coupons sont payables sans retenue d'aucune sorte, tous impôts présents et futurs, tant en France qu'en Égypte, restant à la charge de la Société.

LE PRÉSIDENT DU CONSEIL D'ADMINISTRATION,

Le Caire, le 1er Juillet 1906.

PAR DÉLÉGATION DU CONSEIL D'ADMINISTRATION,

shareholder of the Societe General des Sucreries et de la Rafinnerie, gave the welcome speech.

Impressed with what he saw, the Khedive responded by reading out an imperial firman conferring on Suarès the Ottoman Grand Order of the Medjidieh First Class.

"Votre nom, Monsieur Suarès, est étroitement uni a toutes les entreprises utiles du pays. Je suis heureux de vous éxprimer publiquement ma gratitude en vous conferant la premiere classe de la Medjidieh."

By this deed, the Khedive acclaimed more than just the rejuvenation of Egypt's sugar industry — the country's second largest single employer after cotton. Abbas Hilmi II knew only too well how the Suarèses had been to some extent responsible for other major agro-industrial concerns which followed the creation of the Aswan and Qena dams.

Acknowledged as Egypt's leading real-estate tycoons, the Suarès brothers owned large chunks of land in what was originally called Ismailia, a district of Cairo stretching from Midan al-Opera to Midan Ismail (today, Midan al-Tahrir). The Suarès bank itself was located behind the Credit Foncier Bank, in a wing of the Suarès Building that faced one of the city's principal squares. It therefore came as no surprise when the square was named Rondpoint Suarès, a name which remained in use even after it was re-christened Midan Moustafa Kamel in honor of Egypt's first nationalist whose statue graces the square to this day.

This new moneyed class was not the unique result of Egypt's 'first' privatization efforts. Whole new cadres of white-collar workers and executives also came on stream thanks to a now affordable western education.

Come to replace the liberal economic period was a national bourgeoisie from among the ranks of the 1919 revolution, "Young Egyptians" many of whom owed their well-being to the Daira Sanieh privatization. One of them, Talaat Harb Pasha, who had openly aligned himself with many of the "foreigners", belonged to that emerging class of Egyptian taipans. It was primarily because of his earlier association with the Suarèses, and by fronting for the likes of former Finance Minister Youssef Cattaui Pasha, himself a Suarès son-in-law, that Harb ultimately co-launched Banque Misr and its associated group of companies earning himself the sobriquet of "Father of Egyptian commercial enterprise".

Compagnie des Chemins de Fer Économiques de L'Est Égyptien

Founded in 1897 by Felix Suares whose family dominated almost half the transport business in Egypt.

The concession was to build and operate narrow gauge railways with electric or steam traction in the provinces of Charkieh, Dakahlieh and Kalioubieh. The lines at issuance date extended 350 kilometers.

Capital:
£200,000, each of the 12,500 bonds were worth £20 or FF 504 and yielded a fixed guaranteed interest of 3½% which were exceptionally payable and/or redeemable in gold. It was liquidated before 1938.

COMPAGNIE DES

Chemins de Fer Économiques DE L'EST ÉGYPTIEN

Société Anonyme

Au Capital de £ 200.000

Autorisée par Décret khédivial du 8 Juin 1897.

SIÈGE SOCIAL AU CAIRE

ÉMISSION DE 12.500 OBLIGATIONS DE 504 FRANCS

Représentant un Capital de 6.300 000 francs

3 ½ %

OBLIGATION AU PORTEUR DE Cinq Cent Quatre Francs

ISSUE OF 12.500 BONDS OF £ 20 EACH

Representing a total capital of £ 250.000

3 ½ %

BOND TO BEARER FOR Twenty Pounds Sterling

N° 08,174

INTÉRÊT 17 Fr. 64 PAYABLE EN OR

8 *fr.* 82 *le 1er Janvier et* 8 *fr.* 82 *le 1er Juillet.*

REMBOURSEMENT AU PAIR, EN OR, AU PLUS TARD EN 70 ANNÉES, PAR VOIE DE TIRAGES AU SORT ANNUELS

Le paiement des Coupons et le remboursement des Titres amortis aura lieu : en or, au CAIRE, ALEXANDRIE, PARIS, LONDRES, AMSTERDAM, BRUXELLES et GENÈVE

INTEREST £ 0.14.0 PAYABLE IN GOLD

£ 0.7.0 *on January 1st* £ 0.7.0 *on July 1st*

REDEEMABLE IN GOLD, AT PAR, AND BY ANNUAL DRAWINGS WITHIN A MAXIMUM PERIOD OF 70 YEARS

The interest Coupons and drawn Bonds shall be paid, in gold, at CAIRO, ALEXANDRIA, PARIS, LONDON, AMSTERDAM, BRUSSELS and GENEVA.

Le Caire, le 1er Juillet 1897.

VU : POUR CONTROLE, COUNTERSIGNED

DEUX ADMINISTRATEURS, TWO DIRECTORS

The House of Cattaui

On 21 December 1950, a landmark auction took place in a large neo-Gothic villa at No. 8 Ibrahim Pasha Naguib Street, Garden City. One of the social and intellectual highlights of the Cairo season, the event consisted of auctioning off the extraordinary library of Senator Joseph Aslan Cattaui Pasha (author of *Coup d'oeil sur la chronologie de la nation Egyptienne*, Plon, Paris, 1931) now dead for almost nine years. Cairo's primo auctioneer, Maurice George Lee (formerly Levi) presided over the occasion with the able assistance of rare books expert I. Feldman who had come over especially from Europe.

As priceless books and volumes were finding new homes, the auction signaled the closing of another colonial chapter in Egypt's modern history and the going off stage of one of Cairo's most powerful Jewish families.

Their story started over one hundred and fifty years ago.

In the wake of Egypt's modernization, which started with the reign of Mohammed Ali Pasha (r. 1805-48), vast fortunes were conceived in the form of trading houses, banks and real estate empires. How and the way in which they did it shaped the lives of certain families into the great dynasties they became.

The Cattauis were one such clan. From master of the mint under Viceroy Abbas Hilmi I and *sarraf bashi* under Viceroy Said to minister of transport and finance under King Fouad, the Cattauis, a family of *misrayim* Jews from Egypt, held a most privileged place in the country's politics, commerce and society such as few other families in contemporary Egyptian history. Banking and real estate, formed the basis of their dynastic fortune. Their power and prestige lasted unchallenged well through the first quarter of the 20th century.

The founder of the dynasty, Yacoub Cattaui Bey (1800-83), was a senior administrator in the Egyptian government and a confidant of viceroys and khedives. He lived in opulent splendor in the fashionable district of Shubra where successive rulers set up residence. Yet, by the time he passed away, the seat of power had already shifted to the area of Abdin and the new Cairo district of Ismailia, so named after its promoter, Khedive Ismail Pasha.

Yacoub Cattaui's progeny was large, with two of his four sons, plus a grandson, attaining the distinguished rank of pasha. As for his daughters and granddaughters, they contracted dynastic marriages with other leading Jewish merchant families in Egypt, thus assuring the predominance of the House of Cattaui.

Moise (sometimes called Moussa or Maurice depending on circumstance), was the founder's youngest son. He carried the Ottoman title of pasha as well as a hereditary Hungarian knighthood hence the appendage 'de' in his branch of the family. Like his father before him, Moise made several contributions towards the enhancement of Austrian influence in Egypt thus assuring himself the continued support of a very appreciative European sovereign and protector.

Several Cattaui descendants served in the Egyptian civil service whether as cabinet ministers and senators or,

The Land Bank of Egypt

Authorized by the Khedivial Decree of January 10, 1905 with the right to operate for 99 years to grant loans for mortgages — repayable either at long or short terms and with optional redemption — to estates owners in Egypt. It also purchased mortgage debts and opened current account credits on mortgages. To meet the annual requirements of cultivators and landowners, it advanced cash on a non-mortgage basis within the value of the profits yielded by the land, and cashed their bills to order against endorsment.

Head Office: 13 Talaat Harb Pasha Street, Alexandria.

Capital:
£975,000 divided into 195,000 Ordinary shares of £5 each, fully paid.
£25,000 in 5,000 Founders shares of £5 each.

THE LAND BANK OF EGYPT

Titre au Porteur de UNE Action Ordinaire N° 172,201

THE LAND BANK OF EGYPT

The Land Bank of Egypt

BANQUE FONCIÈRE D'ÉGYPTE

SOCIÉTÉ ANONYME

Créée par Décret Khédivial du 10 Janvier 1905.

CAPITAL : £st. 1.000.000

REPRÉSENTÉ PAR

195.000 Actions Ordinaires de £st. 5 chacune

ET

5.000 Parts de Fondateurs de £st. 5 chacune.

TITRE AU PORTEUR

DE

UNE Action Ordinaire de £st. 5.

Le Porteur du présent titre est propriétaire de **UNE** Action Ordinaire de Cinq Livres Sterling, entièrement libérée, de la Société susdite, portant le numéro indiqué ci-bas, et soumise aux clauses et conditions des Statuts dont un extrait est donné d'autre part.

بنك الأراضي المصري

شركة مساهمة

موسسه بامر عال خديوى صادر بتاريخ ١٠ ينایر سنه ١٩٠٥

الرسمال ١٠٠٠٠٠٠ جنيه

مولف من

١٩٥٠٠٠ سهم عادي قيمة كل سهم خمسة جنيه انجليزي و ٥٠٠٠

سهم تاسيس قيمة كل منهم خمسة جنيه انجليزي ايضا

سند بيد رافعه

عن سهم واحد عادي قيمته خمسة جنيه انجليزي مدفوع بالكمله

حامل هذا السند يمتلك سهم عادي واحد قيمته خمسة جنيه انجليزي

مدفوعين بالكمليه من اسهم الشركه المذكوره تحت النمره الموضحه ادناه

وطبقا للشروط لايحة الشركه الاتي بيان ملخصها

THE LAND BANK OF EGYPT

COMPANY OF LIMITED LIABILITY

Created by Khedivial Decree of the 10th January 1905.

CAPITAL : £st. 1.000.000

REPRESENTED BY

195.000 Ordinary Shares of £st. 5 each

AND

5.000 Deferred Shares of £st. 5 each.

SHARE WARRANT TO BEARER

FOR

ONE Ordinary Share of £st. 5.

This is to certify that the bearer of this Warrant is entitled to **ONE** fully paid Ordinary Share of Five Pounds Sterling in the above Company numbered as above subject to the Statutes of the Company of which an extract is endorsed hereon.

UNE Action Ordinaire N° 172,201

UN ADMINISTRATEUR, | UN ADMINISTRATEUR,

Titre de l'émission du 7 Décembre 1905,
échangé et délivré sous le Sceau de la Banque, à Alexandrie, le

G. FRAIPONT

IMPRIMERIE CHAIX, RUE BERGÈRE, 20, PARIS. — 23034 bis.-11-29. — (Encre Lorilleux).

TALON DES COUPONS DE L'ACTION N° 172,201

Lorsque tous les coupons ci-attachés seront payés ou annoncés pour paiement, la Société, contre remise de ce talon, délivrera au porteur une nouvelle feuille de coupons.

After all the attached coupons have been paid or advertised for payment the Company will on surrender of this Talon issue to the Bearer a fresh Sheet of coupons.

THE LAND BANK OF EGYPT COUPON DE DIVIDENDE N° 50 SUR UNE ACTION ORDINAIRE N° 172,201 Payable en Égypte, à Londres et à Paris.	THE LAND BANK OF EGYPT COUPON DE DIVIDENDE N° 49 SUR UNE ACTION ORDINAIRE N° 172,201 Payable en Égypte, à Londres et à Paris.	THE LAND BANK OF EGYPT COUPON DE DIVIDENDE N° 48 SUR UNE ACTION ORDINAIRE N° 172,201 Payable en Égypte, à Londres et à Paris.	THE LAND BANK OF EGYPT COUPON DE DIVIDENDE N° 47 SUR UNE ACTION ORDINAIRE N° 172,201 Payable en Égypte, à Londres et à Paris.	THE LAND BANK OF EGYPT COUPON DE DIVIDENDE N° 46 SUR UNE ACTION ORDINAIRE N° 172,201 Payable en Égypte, à Londres et à Paris.
THE LAND BANK OF EGYPT COUPON DE DIVIDENDE N° 45 SUR UNE ACTION ORDINAIRE	THE LAND BANK OF EGYPT COUPON DE DIVIDENDE N° 44 SUR UNE ACTION ORDINAIRE	THE LAND BANK OF EGYPT COUPON DE DIVIDENDE N° 43 SUR UNE ACTION ORDINAIRE	THE LAND BANK OF EGYPT COUPON DE DIVIDENDE N° 42 SUR UNE ACTION ORDINAIRE	THE LAND BANK OF EGYPT COUPON DE DIVIDENDE N° 41 SUR UNE ACTION ORDINAIRE

alternately, as deputies from the Upper Egyptian district of Kom-Ombo where the Cattauis held significant interests in the sugar industry.

There were also Cattaui architects, lawyers, poets, musicians and diplomats. One of the latter, George Cattaui, was invariably the chargé at the Royal Egyptian Embassy in the choice posts of London, Paris and Washington. There were also those who spent their time in the pursuit of philanthropy and pleasure as well as the odd man out who broke with family ranks by converting to Catholicism, ultimately becoming a prince of the church.

And they were also the presidents of Egypt's thriving Jewish community.

As for the Cattaui women, they were the leaders and arbitrators of the social scene. They organized glittering court balls, opera premieres and countless charity bazaars. In stark contrast to the traditionally-minded Egyptian upper class women most of whom were never seen in public, early this century the Cattaui consorts were an integral part of Cairo and Alexandria's cosmopolitan societies enhanced by their European education and their emancipated upbringing.

No wonder the Cattaui ladies were seen at all the important premieres as it was their husbands who at one time ran the opera's artistic committee. Al-Ahram of 19 November 1900 lists the committee members as: Prince Hussein Kamel (future sultan of Egypt); Sir Elwin Palmer of the National Bank of Egypt; De Martino Pasha, head of the Privy Council; Comte de Serionne, director of the Suez Canal Company; Moussa Cattaui Bey, Monsieur Raphael Suarès, Youssef Cattaui Bey and Monsieur Ambrosio Sinadino.

At court, several Cattaui relations played important roles. Diplomat-author George Adolphe Cattaui was King Fouad's speechwriter. The wife of Joseph Aslan Cattaui Pasha reigned supreme yielding more influence amongst the courtiers than the queen herself. Known as "Madame Cattaui Pasha", the grande dame of the royal court was born Alice Suarès, daughter of real estate mogul Joseph M. Suarès.

Madame Cattaui Pasha had replaced her late cousin Valentine as first lady-in-waiting to the queen. Valentine, daughter of railway baron Felix Suarès, through her mother was the great granddaughter of the founder of the Cattaui dynasty. Her husband Robert Rolo (later Sir Robert) was the private financial advisor to King Fouad. Heir to a rich merchant house with branches in Cairo, Alexandria, Liverpool and Manchester, Rolo and his anglophile kin were involved in the Manchester and colonial trade evolving into the owners of a powerful private bank.

The Cattauis, the Rolos, the Suarès and their millionaire relation Elie Mosseri Bey (son of Elena Yacoub Cattaui) foresaw the unparalleled growth of Cairo and the lucrative effect such expansion would have on land values. Their separate private residences were located at the nexus of the elegant European quarter of Ismailia and later in the choicest parts of Kasr al-Dubara, Garden City, Zamalek and Giza. For example, the Moise Cattaui residence on Cherifein Street (No. 4) was situated in the middle of a large garden overlooking what we know today as Talaat Harb Square.

Société Viticole et Vinicole d'Égypte

Registered on May 18, 1936 to acquire the activities of the Fondation Gianaclis (N. Pierrakos and Co.) The company cultivates vines and manufactures wine and spirits.

Mr. Nicolas Pierrakos, the managing director, owned the majority of the share capital of the company.

Originally, the company owned an area of 4,432 feddans of which 1,080 were occupied by vineyards. The land is situated near the village of Gianaclis, in upper Mariut, about 25 kilometres from the Mediterranean, west of Alexandria. In November 1944, the company purchased from the Societé Gianaclis Limited a further 2,923 feddans between the Nubarieh Canal and the company's estate. Another 837 feddans were exchanged for a similar area on payment of a difference of L.E. 15,000. These acquisitions assured its independence for the irrigation water required for its vineyards and other crops. In 1946, the total area of the company's estate comprised 7,355 feddans.

Head Office: 5 Borsa Street (Tewfikieh), Cairo.

Capital:
L.E. 500,000 divided into 125,000 Ordinary shares of L.E. 4 each, fully paid.

5 ACTIONS

Titre N° 15244

شركة الكروم والكحول المصرية

شركة مساهمة مصرية

مرخص بانشائها بموجب مرسوم ملكي صادر في ٦ مايو سنة ١٩٣٦

قانونها الأساسي مسجل في قلم كتاب محكمة مصر التجارية المختلطة بتاريخ ٢٨ مايو سنة ١٩٣٦ تحت رقم ١٣٨ جزء ٣٩ صفحة ١٠٧ ونشر بالجريدة الرسمية بتاريخ ١٨ مايو سنة ١٩٣٦ وعدلته الجمعية العمومية في الجلسات غير العادية المنعقدة في ٢٥ مايو و٢٤ يوليو سنة ١٩٣٦ و ٣ مارس سنة ١٩٣٧ و ٢٧ سبتمبر سنة ١٩٤٤

Société Viticole et Vinicole d'Egypte

SOCIÉTÉ ANONYME EGYPTIENNE

AUTORISÉE PAR DÉCRET ROYAL DU 6 MAI 1936

STATUTS ENREGISTRÉS AU GREFFE COMMERCIAL MIXTE DU CAIRE LE 28 MAI 1936 SUB No. 138 VOL. 39 FOL. 107

PUBLIÉS AU JOURNAL OFFICIEL DU 18 MAI 1936 ET MODIFIÉS PAR LES ASSEMBLÉES GÉNÉRALES EXTRAORDINAIRES DU 25 MAI, DU 24 JUILLET 1936, DU 3 MARS 1937 ET DU 27 SEPTEMBRE 1944

رأس المال ٥٠٠,٠٠٠ جنيه مصري

موزع على ١٢٥,٠٠٠ سهم قيمة كل منها ٤ جنيهات مصرية ودفعت قيمتها كاملة

CAPITAL SOCIAL L.E. 500.000

REPRÉSENTÉ PAR 125.000 ACTIONS DE LIVRES EGYPTIENNES QUATRE CHACUNE ENTIÈREMENT LIBÉRÉES

المركز الرئيسي بالقاهرة

SIÈGE SOCIAL AU CAIRE

خمسة اسهم لحامله قيمة كل منها اربعة جنيهات مصرية

CINQ ACTIONS AU PORTEUR DE L.Eg. QUATRE CHACUNE

N° 78466 à N° 78470

رئيس مجلس الادارة — LE PRÉSIDENT DU CONSEIL D'ADMINISTRATION

LE CAIRE, NOVEMBRE 1944 القاهرة نوفمبر سنة ١٩٤٤

احد اعضاء مجلس الادارة — UN ADMINISTRATEUR

In its early days, Kasr al-Nil Street was often referred to as rue Cattaui. In fact, this section of Cairo boasted two Cattaui streets: rue Cattaui and rue Moise Cattaui Pasha. There were Cattaui streets in other parts of Cairo as well such as the Cattaui Street that ran from Midan Khazindar to Sharia Rouei and the Moussa Cattaui Bey Street in Abbassia.

Julius Franz Pasha built the original downtown Moise de Cattaui Pasha palace No. 23 Kasr al-Nil Street. A large garden and an equally large pond surrounded it. The house was redesigned in 1907 by the architectural firm of (Maurice) Cattaui & Edward Matasek to make way for a much larger residence.

The 19 May 1924 obituary of Moussa Cattaui Pasha in al-Ahram reports:

"Come to pay their respects were a large number of dignitaries both foreign and Egyptian. Apart from the King's representative, present at the funeral were incumbent Prime Minister Saad Zaghloul Pasha accompanied by two former head of governments, Adly Yegen Pasha and Tewfik Nessim Pasha. Also present were the President of the Chamber Ahmed Mazloum Pasha and [future prime minister] Ahmed Ziwar Pasha. From the ruling house were Princes Mohammed-Ali Tewfik [brother of the former Khedive of Egypt] and Kamal al-Din Hussein [son of the late Sultan of Egypt]. Eulogies were read by publisher Leon Castro, Mr. Henri Naus Bey director of the Sugar Company, Mr. Adda chairman of the Ecoles Israelites, Osman Murtada Pasha former governor of Alexandria and Mr. Abramino Menasha head of a variety of Jewish charity organizations."

In 1927, Cattaui's Kasr al-Nil property was sold and the house torn down to make way for a collection of buildings foremost among them is the Shell Building and the Cairo Bourse.The section of the garden facing Midan Soliman Pasha (later Talaat Harb) was also sacrificed to commercial development. It was there that the Sednaoui building designed by Giuseppe Mazza was constructed.

To the south of the large Moise Cattaui townhouse stood the houses and offices of other Cattaui relations such as the marble villa on Kasr al-Nil Street belonging to Youssef Yacoub Cattaui Pasha and his wife Bida Eliahou Israel, the daughter and granddaughter of Cairo and Jerusalem's 19th century grand rabbis. After the death of Bida Israel Cattaui in June 1922, the house was pulled down and what remained of the garden with its royal palms and red gravel paths was taken over by Sault's, then a favorite tea room and café-restaurant.

Further north, towards Avenue Fouad (today 26th of July Street), lived Nessim Mosseri with his wife Elena Yacoub Cattaui. Their residence occupied almost an entire block fronting today's 26 of July and Mohamed Farid Streets. It is said the Mosseris donated part of their garden for the construction of the Ismailia Synagogue on Maghrabi (now Adly) Street. The synagogue, which was designed by Cattaui & Matasek, was the scene of many Cattaui weddings and funerals. As for the Nessim Mosseri house, it became Cairo's first museum of modern art.

Another Cattaui residence worth mentioning is Youssef Aslan Cattaui Pasha's turreted neo-Gothic villa attributed to architects Matasek and Cattaui. Contiguous to the palace of Princess Nimet Kamal al Dine (today the Ministry

Credit Agricole d'Égypte

Created by Royal Decree on 25 July 1931 to advance short term loans, for periods not exceeding 14 months, to small farmers and agricultural co-operative societies enabling them to cultivate their land and collect the crop. The bank also sells fertilisers on cash or credit terms and grants loans against agricultural produce. Loans for longer periods, ranging from 3 to 10 years, were granted for the purchase of agricultural machinery and farm animals and for land improvements.

Head Office: 11 Gameh Charkass Street, Cairo.

Capital:
L.E. 1,000,000 represented by 250,000 Ordinary shares of L.E. 4 each, fully paid.
Half of the capital was subscribed by the Egyptian Governemnt and the other half by leading banking and financial institutions in Egypt. In accordance with Law no. 50 of 1930, the Egyptian Government was authorized to advance funds to the Bank up to a maximum of L.E. 6,000,000 at a low interest rate. The Government guaranteed shareholders an annual dividend of 5 per cent.

ACTIONS 10

بنك التسليف الزراعى المصرى

سهم ١٠

شركة مساهمة مصرية مركزها القاهرة

صادر بتأسيسها مرسوم ملكى بتاريخ ٢٥ يوليه سنة ١٩٣١

برأس مال اولى مقداره ١,٠٠٠,٠٠٠ جنيه اشتركت الحكومة فى نصفه
موزع على ٢٥٠,٠٠٠ سهم قيمة كل سهم اربعة جنيهات مصرية
مدفوعة بالكلها وضمنت الحكومة لأسهم رأس المال الاصلى ربحاً قدره ٥٪

CREDIT AGRICOLE D'EGYPTE

SOCIETE ANONYME EGYPTIENNE

Siège Social: LE CAIRE

AUTORISÉE PAR DÉCRET ROYAL EN DATE DU 25 JUILLET 1931

CAPITAL ORIGINAIRE L.E. 1.000.000 DONT MOITIÉ SOUSCRITE PAR LE GOUVERNEMENT.
DIVISÉ EN 250.000 ACTIONS DE L.E. 4 CHACUNE, ENTIÈREMENT VERSÉES.
LE GOUVERNEMENT GARANTIT UN DIVIDENDE DE 5% AUX ACTIONS DU CAPITAL ORIGINAIRE.

Dix Actions au porteur d'une valeur de L.E. 40 (Quarante Livres Egyptiennes) entièrement libérées. Les clauses et conditions des statuts de la Banque, dont un extrait est imprimé au verso, sont applicables au porteur.

عشرة أسهم لحاملها قيمتها أربعون جنيهاً مصرياً مدفوعة بالكلها ويكون حاملها خاضعاً لأحكام وشروط البنك المدرج مستخرج منها فى ظهر هذا

Le Président du Conseil d'Administration

رئيس مجلس الادارة

Un Administrateur

عضو مجلس الادارة

Nº 71971 AUNº 71980

رقم ٧١٩٧١ الى ٧١٩٨٠

Le Caire, le 1er. Novembre 1934

القاهرة فى اول نوفمبر ١٩٣٤

L.E. 40

جنيه مصرى ٤٠

IMPRIMERIE MISR, S.A.E., LE CAIRE, EGYPTE.

of Foreign Affairs) in the east, the villa stood at the eastern entrance of Kasr al Nil Bridge. When Joseph Cattaui moved to his newly commissioned neo-Gothic villa in Garden City circa 1920, the older villa was purchased by Kout al-Kouloub al-Demerdashia. In the 1960s, it was torn down to make way for a circular ramp/access road leading on to Kasr al-Nil Bridge.

The palatial Cattaui homes were centers of entertainment and hospitality. A Cattaui wedding inevitably led to traffic congestion while the death of one of Yacoub Cattaui's male descendants led to the closure of the Cairo or Alexandria Bourse.

In Charles Didier's book *Les Nuits du Caire* (1860), we learn of a *brit mila*, or circumcision fête that took place at Kasr al Nozha, the Cattaui palace in Shubra. The eight-day old boy was Yacoub Cattaui's youngest son, Moise. According to Didier, everyone was in native dress and since no one knew French save for a very few, the conversation amongst the invited notables was conducted in either Turkish or Arabic. We also learn that women were nowhere in sight. As customary, they were celebrating in another quarter of the opulent palace entertained by the diva of the day, the Oriental singer Sakna and her accompanying *taar* or drum.

Twenty-six years after his circumcision, it was the turn for Moise's newly born son, Gustave, to undergo the same ceremony. Present at these celebrations was Khedive Ismail himself. The difference this time was that the festivities were attended by both sexes and that in the course of one generation, the language of conversation had shifted from Arabic to French. The irreversible Europeanization of the Cattauis and a whole generation of Cairo's Levantine community had begun in earnest thanks to the Paris-based Alliance Israelite Universelle and to French cultural imperialism that had so imbued Egypt at the end of the 19th century.

Even before Moise married his European wife Ida Rossi, French had not only displaced Italian in the Mixed Courts, but had also become the lingua franca of the entire business community.

When the Earl of Dufferin, the British Ambassador to the Sublime Porte in Constantinople, visited Egypt in 1882, he stayed in the Cattaui palace. This was the ultimate honor for the host since Egypt at the time was still an Ottoman province.

To fathom the scale of entertainment that went on at the Cattaui homes, one refers to the 28 May 1909 edition of Le Progrés, which illustrates in detail the 11-course dinner offered by Moise and Ida Cattaui when entertaining the visiting Austrian Minister. The guests were limited to 16 because Ida was in mourning over the loss of her father, Elia Rossi Bey, the former doctor of the Khedivial court and author of the book *La Nubia e il Sudan*.

From the Egyptian Gazette (1905), we note that Moise de Cattaui Pasha's extensive real estate holdings included the 6,000 square metres of Nile frontage in the fashionable district of Kasr al-Dubara. He sold it to the Swiss hotelier Mr. Bucher-Durrer for five pounds sterling a square metre so that the latter could erect his Edwardian-style Semiramis Hotel (today replaced by the Semiramis-Intercontinental).

Chemins de fer de la Basse-Egypte

Registered on January 26, 1886. The company held a 70-year concession from the Egyptian Government to operate a railway in the Dakahlia province of Lower Egypt. The concession was to expire on June 30, 1964, with all the lines reverting to the Government without compensation. The Basse-Egypte Line was the first light railway line to be constructed in the Delta, opening to traffic on September 28, 1897. The total length of lines on June 30, 1955 was 257 kilometers. The Mataria–Mansourah and Mansourah–Damietta lines fromed the principal sections of the railway.

Head Office: 1 Maspero Street (Boulac), Cairo.

Capital:
L.E. 293,170 in 15,200 Preference shares of E.Fr. 500 each to be redeemed at E.Fr. 600. Of the total shares issued, 1,592 were redeemed and converted into Jouissance shares.
1,592 Jouissance shares.
14,000 Dividend shares of no pa

Une nouvelle feuille de coupons comprenant 20 coupons n° 21 au 40 du 1er novembre 1917 au 1er novembre 1936 a été délivrée.

SOCIÉTÉ ANONYME

DES

Chemins de fer de la Basse-Egypte

Autorisée par décret de S. A. le Khédive, *en date du* 26 *janvier* 1896

CAPITAL SOCIAL : 3,500,000 FRANCS

Représenté par 7,000 actions privilégiées de 500 francs chacune et 14,000 actions de dividende sans désignation de valeur.

ACTION PRIVILÉGIÉE DE 500 FRANCS AU PORTEUR

N° 1859

REMBOURSABLE PAR 600 FRANCS

Le Caire, le 15 mars 1896

UN ADMINISTRATEUR, UN ADMINISTRATEUR,

Le décret autorisant la constitution de la Société, l'acte de constitution, les statuts approuvés, ont été publiés en supplément au journal égyptien du 27 janvier 1896; ces mêmes documents, l'acte de concession et le cahier des charges du tramway à voie étroite, à traction à vapeur, de Mansourah à Matarieh, ont été publiés dans le recueil spécial des actes et documents relatifs aux Sociétés, annexes au *Moniteur belge* du 5 mars 1896 et suivant.

Bruxelles. — Imprimerie typo. et lithographique Ve Monnom, rue de l'Industrie

To the southeast of the Semiramis Hotel were several stately villas belonging to Cattaui relations. One belonged to Sir Robert Rolo. In the 1950s it became the (USIA) American Embassy Library before it was destroyed by fire. Today the land on which it stood forms an integral part of the fort-like American Embassy compound .

One of the more prominent and mediatized members of his family, Joseph Aslan Cattaui Pasha started off as an engineer after completing his studies in the Ecole Central in France in 1882. Upon returning to Egypt, he worked in the ministry of public works where he participated in a competition for the design of the Alexandria Railway Station. He then joined the administration of the sugar factories in Upper Egypt belonging to his Suarès relations. It was with that purpose in mind that he traveled to Moravia to learn about sugar refining. With time, Joseph Cattaui Pasha became a director of both the Sucreries d'Égypte and the Kom-Ombo Sugar Company. He also joined Egypt's 33rd government headed by Ahmed Ziwar Pasha in November 1924 and then again in the 34th government of March 1926. In 1927, King Fouad appointed him to the senate.

Between 1924 and 1942, Joseph Cattaui Pasha was president of the Sephardi Jewish Council of Cairo, a post which heretofore had been occupied by his uncle, Moise Cattaui Pasha. A self-declared anti-Zionist, Joseph Pasha stood firm on the issue, which made him unpopular with some of the more radical elements within his community.

Upon Joseph Pasha's death, his son René took over the presidency of the Jewish Community until his induced resignation in 1946. For the first time in almost half a century, a Cattaui was no longer in control despite his lineage and strong boardroom connections.

Aside from their handsome residences, the Cattauis owned large chunks of real estate in and around Cairo. Among them is Les Halles or indoor marketplace on Midan Falaki, Bab al-Louk that was built in 1911 on newly acquired Cattaui property. Joseph and Adolphe Cattaui owned the Société des Halles Centrales d'Égypte.

In the district of Abbassia, the Cattauis owned masses of property, possibly acquired when Yacoub Cattaui Bey was master of the mint to Abbas I. It was from this land that Yacoub donated a sizable plot to the Austro-Hungarian community in 1881 for the erection of the first Crown Prince Rudolf Hospital. Although the hospital was inaugurated on 2 December 1888 on the occasion of Franz Josef's 40th anniversary as Emperor of Austria, it would be 23 years later before Moise Yacoub Cattaui Pasha, president of the Austro-Hungarian colony since 1906, received his Hungarian letters of nobility entitling him to the appendage of "de" to his name: henceforth known as Moise de Cattaui.

The Israelite school which opened in 1920 near Fagalah on Sakakini Street was named after its benefactor, Moise de Cattaui Pasha. A decade earlier, on 20 May 1909, he had inaugurated another Israelite school on Hassan al-Akbar Street, opposite the Khedivial Law School. In 1927, the large Israelite school of Abbassia was inaugurated thanks to generous donations from Joseph Aslan Cattaui Pasha and other members of the Jewish community.

In Giza, the Cattaui-Mosseri-owned Cairo Land & Financial Company acquired the palace and the adjacent

Astra & Halles Centrales d'Égypte

In November 1944, the Societe Anonyme des Halles Centrales d'Egypre (registered in 1911) and the Astra Milk Co. (founded in 1924) merged.

The new company owned a diary farm at the Pyramids near Cairo where pasteurized milk, cream cheese, butter, eggs and other dairy products were produced under hygienic conditions. These were sold to the public through a number of retail establishments (also serving as Milk Bars) owned by the company of which eight were in Cairo, one at Heliopolis, four in Alexandria and one at Ramleh (Alexandria), known as the Mayfair Inn at Stanley Bay.

The company was also engaged in the construction and management of markets. It built a modern vegetable and fruit market on Tewfik Street, in Heliopolis. The new market included 50 shops equipped with a refrigerating plant for the storage of perishable goods.

Head Office: 37 Kasr-el-Nil Street, Cairo.

Capital:
L.E. 120,000 divided into 30,000 Ordinary shares of L.E. 4 each, fully paid. Capital authorized L.E. 150,000.

25 ACTIONS

٢٥ سهما

شركة استرا والأسواق المحلية المصرية

شركة مساهمة مصرية - المركز الرئيسي بالقاهرة

السجل التجاري ١٧٩٦٩

مصرح لها بأمر عال بتاريخ ٢٠ مارس سنة ١٩١١ ونشر بالجريدة الرسمية عدد ٣٤ بتاريخ ٢٧ مارس سنة ١٩١١

تعلى رأس مالها إلى ١٥٠٠٠٠ جنيها مصريًا

يوزع على ٣٧٥٠٠ سهم قيمة السهم الواحد أربعة جنيهات مصرية بموجب قرار الجمعية الغير عادية بتاريخ ٣٠ نوفمبر سنة ١٩٤٤

خمسة وعشرون سهما لحاملها قيمة السهم الواحد أربعة جنيهات مصرية دفعت كاملة

ASTRA & HALLES CENTRALES D'EGYPTE

SOCIETE ANONYME EGYPTIENNE — SIEGE SOCIAL: LE CAIRE

REG.COM.No. 17969, LE CAIRE

Autorisée par Décret Khédivial du 20 Mars 1911 promulgué au Journal Officiel No. 34 du 27 Mars 1911

CAPITAL SOCIAL AUGMENTE A L.E. 150.000

Divisé en 37.500 Actions au Porteur de L.E. 4 chacune

Suivant Décision de l'Assemblée Générale Extraordinaire du 30 Novembre 1944

VINGT-CINQ ACTIONS AU PORTEUR de L.E. Quatre chacune entièrement libérées.

عضو مجلس الإدارة
Un Administrateur

عضو مجلس الإدارة
Un Administrateur

ASTRA & HALLES CENTRALES D'EGYPTE

N° 12601 à N° 12625

Le Caire, le Novembre 1944

١٠٠ جنيه مصري

L.E. 100

25 شركة استرا والأسواق المحلية المصرية ٢٥	24 شركة استرا والأسواق المحلية المصرية ٢٤	23 شركة استرا والأسواق المحلية المصرية ٢٣	22 شركة استرا والأسواق المحلية المصرية ٢٢	21 شركة استرا والأسواق المحلية المصرية ٢١
ASTRA & HALLES CENTRALES D'EGYPTE	ASTRA & HALLES CENTRALES D'EGYPTE	ASTRA & HALLES CENTRALES D'EGYPTE	ASTRA & HALLES CENTRALES D'EGYPTE	ASTRA & HALLES CENTRALES D'EGYPT
VINGT CINQ ACTIONS خمسة وعشرون سهما	VINGT CINQ ACTIONS خمسة وعشرون سهما	VINGT CINQ ACTIONS خمسة وعشرون سهما	VINGT CINQ ACTIONS خمسة وعشرون سهما	VINGT CINQ ACTIONS خمسة وعشرون سهما
N° 12601 à N° 12625	N° 12601 à N° 12625	N° 12601 à N° 12625	N° 12601 à N° 12625	N° 12601 à N° 12625
25 COUPON PAYABLE AU PORTEUR كوبون يدفع لحامله ٢٥	24 COUPON PAYABLE AU PORTEUR كوبون يدفع لحامله ٢٤	23 COUPON PAYABLE AU PORTEUR كوبون يدفع لحامله ٢٣	22 COUPON PAYABLE AU PORTEUR كوبون يدفع لحامله ٢٢	21 COUPON PAYABLE AU PORTEUR كوبون يدفع لحامله

property belonging to Sultan Hussein Kamel. It is there that several Cattaui-Mosseris built their mansions when they moved out of downtown Cairo. One of the remaining villas belongs today to the Russian Embassy. Another one (behind the Russian Embassy), once the property of Victor Mosseri, became a government school still recognizable for its gargoyles and other Victorian follies.

There was the Alexandria branch as well. Its patriarch, Baron Jacques Bohor Yacoub Levi de Menashe was the son of Semha, Yacoub Cattaui's eldest daughter. The Menashes were amongst the first to take advantage of the blanket protection given to the Jews of that city in 1854 by Austria's monarch. Having caught Emperor Franz Josef's attention during the Suez Canal inaugural celebrations of 1869, Yacoub Levi Menashe, an Alexandrian merchant claiming ancestry in Central Europe, was ennobled by the Austrian Emperor in October 1873. Two years later, the honor was upgraded to the hereditary title of Hungarian Baron. Alexandria's colorful aristocracy thus welcomed yet another nobleman among its inflated ranks. Like their Cattaui cousins in Cairo, the Menashes were the leaders of the Jewish community residing in Egypt's maritime capital.

At the turn of the century the name Menashe was synonymous with power, wealth and arts. The Menashe legacy in Alexandria is abundant starting with the Menashe Gallery, which faces Mohammed Ali Square (ex-Place des Consuls), the Menashe schools, the Menashe hospitals and the Menashe temples. There were also the great Menashe houses, the Menashe immeubles de rapport, and rue Menashe.

In 1904, the Cattauis and the Menashes, together with two influential British financial advisors to the Egyptian government, Sir Auckland Colvin and Sir Elwin Palmer, formed the Egyptian Delta Land & Investment Company, which created in 1907 the suburb of Maadi along the Bab al-Louk–Helwan railway line belonging to a consortium led by Jacob Cattaui's son-in-law, Felix Suarès.

The Delta Land Co. was but one of several urban and agricultural venture capital companies owned by the same business elite made up of Cattauis, Suarès, Menashes and Rolos. Later, Elie Mosseri Bey (grandson of Yacoub Cattaui) whose accumulated wealth made him the undisputed first among equals, would join the conclave.

The founding fathers and early directors of the National Bank of Egypt, which opened in June 1898, included a Cattaui (Moise Pasha), a Menashe (Baron Jacques), two Rolos (Jacob and Sir Robert), and three Suarès (Felix, Raphael and Leon). These gentlemen were either descendants of Yacoub Cattaui or related to him by marriage. But even before the National Bank was created, the Cattauis were directors of several banks and companies in Egypt, a position they retained well into the 1930s.

The Cattauis also had large banking and business dealings in Europe, notably Paris. Leafing through the leading Parisian newspapers of February 1903, one learns of a famous libel suit at the Palais de Justice brought against the celebrated Humberts-Daurignacs of Paris by the "well-known Egyptian banker Monsieur Cattaui whom Madame Frederic Humbert had accused of usury."

Banque Menaché Le Caire

The subject of this deed is a Panama Canal Stock purchased by a hairdresser from Menaché Cousins Bank in 1912 for P.T. 675 divided into 27 installments of P.T. 25 each, the first to be paid upon signature of contract.

Menaché Cousins Bank, established in 1888, joined the private banking activity that the Jews of Egypt excelled at in the thirties and forties. Other examples are the Mosseri Bank (1935); Zilkha Bank (Cairo, 1937; Alxeandria,1940); as well as Banque Suarès and Rofé. All these private banks were engaged in marketing the Panama Canal certificates. All their legal issues were subject to the Mixed Tribunals.

بنك منشي ابناء عم
بمصر

محل مؤسس في سنة ١٨٨٨

العنوان للاشارات البرقية «منشي بمصر»

تحريراً بمصر في ٢٢ يناير سنة ١٩١٧

عن المباع من بنك الخواجات منشي ابناء عم تحت الاحكام الاتي توضيحها

الى جناب علي ابراهيم حلاوه دكان بالقلادنه بدرب الحجاج

المقيم بمصر عنوان بالقلادنه

عدد سند واحد [illegible]

شروط البيع

اولاً — البيع حاصل برضاء وقبول الطرفين بثمن قدره [illegible]

والشيء المباع هو على ذمة المشتري من الآن

ثانياً — الثمن يدفع باعتبار [illegible] وقت تسليم هذا العقد للمشتري ممضي عليه من البائعين والباقي بايصالات شهرية عدد ٢٦ عن كل شهر [illegible]

ثالثاً — قيمة صافي الفوائد المقررة وصافي كل ما يحصل بنسبة الاقتراع من الاوراق بحسب نصيبها في أثناء مدة العقد يصير قيده طلباً للمشتري

رابعاً — نمرة السند المباع يصير درجه بدفتر حسابات البائعين تحت اسم المشتري ويعطى له بياناً وقت تصديق البائعين على هذا العقد بالبيع الصادر منهم

خامساً — باقي الثمن يصير دفعه في بنك الخواجات منشي ابناء عم بمصر ولو كانوا الخواجات المذكورين يرسلوا لسبب تقصير المشتري عن الدفع أو لأي سبب آخر الوصولات لمنزل المشتري لتحصيل الاقساط المتأخرة فهذا الامر لا يكون سبباً للاخلال بأحقيتهم في قبض ما يكون مطلوباً لهم في محل اشغالهم بمصر دون محل اقامة المشتري . وكل ايصال يصدر يلزم ان يكون مشتملاً على نمرة حساب جاري المشتري وموقعاً عليه امضاء بنك الخواجات منشي ابناء عم وختم محلهم والمشتري مكلف برفض أي ايصال مخالفاً لما توضح عنه قبلاً لانه يعتبر عديم القيمة مهما كان الموقع عليه

نرجوكم ان تطلبوا من القومسيونجي بالبيع جواب تفويضه

Madame Humbert was the daughter-in-law of Auguste Humbert, the former French minister of justice. The charges she brought against Monsieur Cattaui were not very favorable to the latter's business reputation. "For me, Cattaui and his son-in-law Mr. Reitlinger, have certainly been the biggest and most terrible usurers who have ever crossed my path. Cattaui was always inexorable, always trying to bleed me for money with his fantastic rates of interest reaching between 300 and 400 per cent." Strong accusation against the 1886 recipient of the French Legion d'Honneur for services rendered to French residents in Egypt. The ensuing court case was among the most notorious of the decade.

The process of gentrification and westernization of the Cattauis, which started in the heyday of Khedive Ismail's reign, was completed with the arrival of Moise de Cattaui Pasha and his generation. By that time, the European powers had carved up what remained of the vast Ottoman Empire taking full advantage of the latter's profitable regime of capitulations or concessions.

During the heyday of Britain's almost 75-year occupation of Egypt, the Cattauis and their relations had become the fulcrum of Egypt's business world. But as is usual with third and fourth generations in comparable dynasties, the Cattaui wealth slowly dissipated through squandering, bad investments, inheritance and taxes. More importantly, the economic and political climate had changed and fierce competition appeared from new and different quarters. The less-motivated Cattaui heirs had come of age and taken over. They lacked the drive, hunger and cutting edge that had made their parents and grandparents such great achievers.

Today, the Cattauis are no longer super rich or omnipotent, just well-heeled citizens leading contented lives. Out of Yacoub Cattaui's many descendants, less than a handful can be found in Egypt; these have adapted well and not so well to changing times. The rest are scattered around the world either as diplomats in European chancelleries, country squires in Scotland, financiers in Geneva or, alternately as auctioneers in New York. There are also the pensioners in Lausanne, the poets in Paris and the artists in Marseille. One of them, Henri Cohen, a grandson of Moise Cattaui, still imports cotton from Egypt.

Electricity & Ice Supply Co.

Registered on August 16, 1906 to acquire the Société d'Electricité d'Isamailia, owners of a concession from the Egyptian Government for the supply of light and power to the town of Ismailia in the Suez Canal Zone. The original concession, which expired on February 17, 1928, was extended until August 17, 1958.

The installed capacity of the generating station was 1,000 k.w. in 4 units, 3-phase current, 50 cycles, 22 volts, supplying over 2,422 consumers for domestic, public and industrial purposes.

The company also owned an ice plant supplying the city of Ismailia. And since October 1934, has been operating a factory producting electric bulbs, sold under the trade name of "Al-Ahram". All the shares of the company are held by a few Swiss citizens.

Head Office: 12 Sidi Metwalli St., Alexandria

Cairo office: 18 Cherif Pasha, St.

Lamp factory: Bahtim, near Cairo.

Capital:
L.E. 88,000 divided into 22,000 Ordinary shares of L.E. 4 each, fully paid.

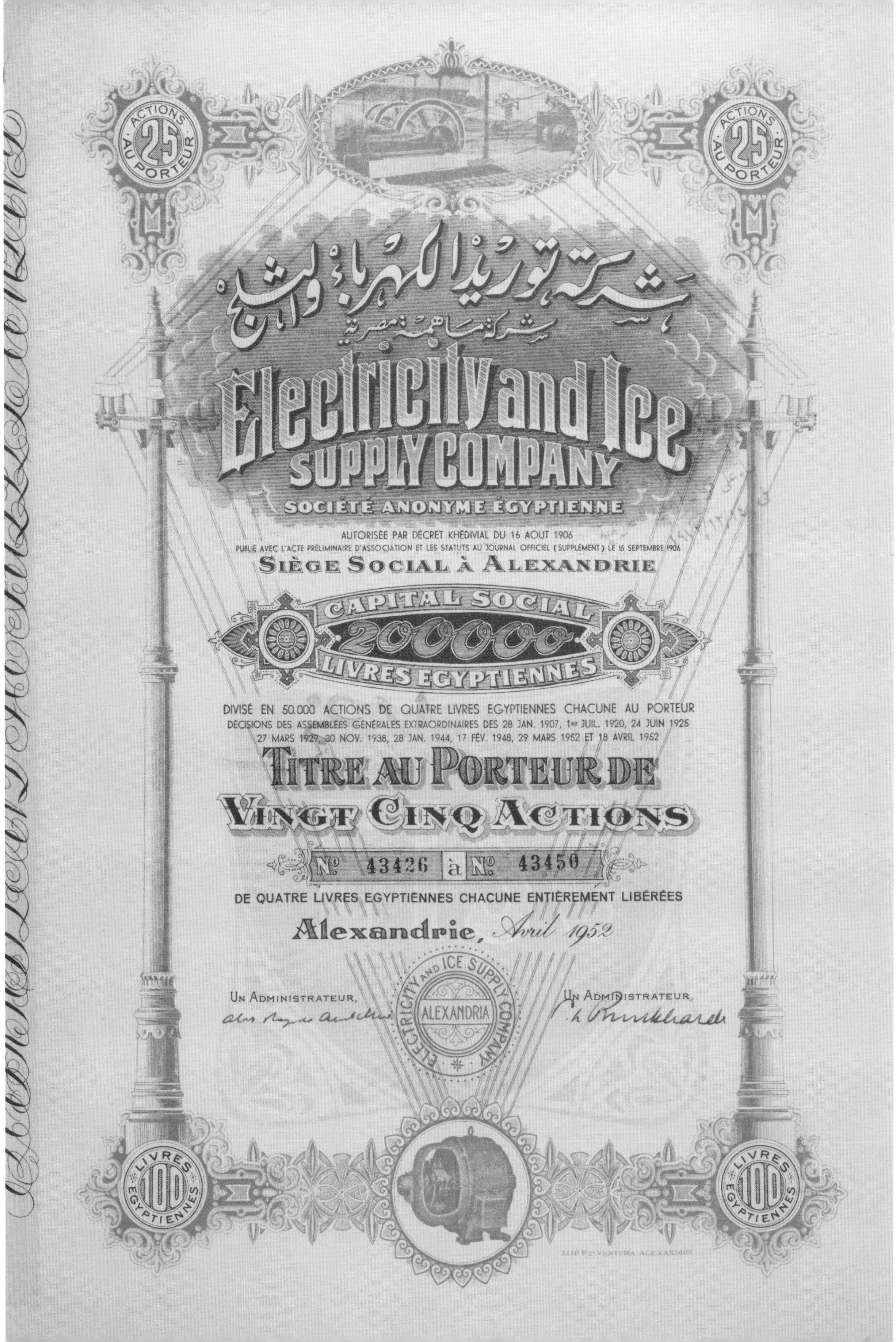

شركة توريد الكهرباء والثلج
شركة مساهمة مصرية

ELECTRICITY AND ICE SUPPLY COMPANY

SOCIÉTÉ ANONYME ÉGYPTIENNE

AUTORISÉE PAR DÉCRET KHÉDIVIAL DU 16 AOUT 1906
PUBLIÉ AVEC L'ACTE PRÉLIMINAIRE D'ASSOCIATION ET LES STATUTS AU JOURNAL OFFICIEL (SUPPLÉMENT) LE 15 SEPTEMBRE 1906

SIÈGE SOCIAL À ALEXANDRIE

CAPITAL SOCIAL 200000 LIVRES EGYPTIENNES

DIVISÉ EN 50.000 ACTIONS DE QUATRE LIVRES EGYPTIENNES CHACUNE AU PORTEUR
DÉCISIONS DES ASSEMBLÉES GÉNÉRALES EXTRAORDINAIRES DES 28 JAN. 1907, 1er JUIL. 1920, 24 JUIN 1925
27 MARS 1929, 30 NOV. 1938, 28 JAN. 1944, 17 FÉV. 1948, 29 MARS 1952 ET 18 AVRIL 1952

TITRE AU PORTEUR DE
VINGT CINQ ACTIONS

Nº 43426 à Nº 43450

DE QUATRE LIVRES EGYPTIENNES CHACUNE ENTIÈREMENT LIBÉRÉES

Alexandrie, Avril 1952

UN ADMINISTRATEUR,

UN ADMINISTRATEUR,

25 ACTIONS AU PORTEUR

100 LIVRES ÉGYPTIENNES

ELECTRICITY AND ICE SUPPLY COMPANY ALEXANDRIA

LITH. Fr. VENTURA - ALEXANDRIE

Constantine and Mikes Salvagos of Alexandria

It was no accident that the National Bank of Egypt's third founding partner fell to Constantine M. Salvagos. At their peak, the Salvagos family controlled over 130,000 feddans of agricultural land, most of it cotton. Privately, they owned over 1,800 prime agricultural feddans in the Delta.

Unlike the thousands of long-term Greek residents of Egypt, the Salvagos were relative late-comers. For several decades, the Greeks of Alexandria formed one of the largest agglomerations outside Greece and the Anatolian peninsula. Come to increase their numbers was one Constantine Salvagos, a textile merchant from the island of Chios by way of Marseilles. He had heard of Egypt's cotton boom prompted in large part by the American Civil War and had come to stake his claim of the spoils. C.M. Salvagos & Co. of Alexandria would see its fortunes multiply further after the 1882 British military occupation of Egypt.

Together with the Choremis, Rodocanachis, Casullis, Sinadinos, Rallis and Benachis, the Salvagos formed the top echelons of the large Greek community of Egypt. Most were in the cotton trade either as growers, ginners, exporters, shippers or bankers. They were also the directors of the all-powerful Alexandria General Produce Association (AGPA), a cartel which regulated all matters pertaining to cotton trade. Their motto: What was good for AGPA was good for Egypt. This was the era of King Cotton.

Constantine Salvagos, and later his heir Mikes, were presidents of six of Egypt's largest land and utility companies in the northern Delta. The most important were Societe Anonyme du Behera founded in 1880 and its offshoot, Union Fonciere d'Égypte founded in 1905. The others were the Alexandria Water Company Limited founded in 1879, the Alexandria & Ramleh Railways Company founded in 1862, the Filature Nationale d'Égypte and the Societe Egyptienne des Industries Textiles.

The Salvagos were also board members or directors of the Egyptian Salt & Soda Company Ltd. (1899); the National Insurance Company of Egypt (1900); the Land Bank of Egypt (1905); the Bank of Abyssinia (1905); the Gabbari Land Company 1907; and the Societe Anonyme de Nettoyage et Pressage de Cotton (1922).

For several generations, a Salvagos presided over the 100,000 strong Greek community of Alexandria, a position they relinquished in 1948 when Mikes Salvagos died at 73. Despite their status, unless you belonged to the Hellenic cream, Greeks were not always in evidence at the great Salvagos residence at No. 6 rue des Ptolemes.

What they lacked in community spirit, the Salvagos made up for in charity works. There was the Salvagos Dispensary, the Salvagos Crafts & Trade School and a number of other Salvagos-backed philanthropic institutions spread all over Alexandria. No one was going to accuse Mikes or Argine Salvagos of parsimony.

Just like the Suarès of Cairo, by the time the Salvagos reached the second and third generations, they had tied the marital knot with most important members of their community, notably the Benachis and Choremis.

The Alexandria & Ramleh Railway Company

Registered in England on June 27, 1883. Until March 31, 1946, it operated the Alexandria Tramways system under a concession from the Municipality for 50 years. At the end of the concession, only the lines and aerial connections reverted to the Municipality without compensation. On April 1, 1946, the Municipality exercised its option to take over the Tramways.

The Tramways system comprised 57 kms of 925 double track and 7 single track, divided into 6 routes. The routes were: Nouzha–Mex (via Ramleh Station); Moharrem Bey–New Customs Zone (via Tewfik St.); Moharrem Bey–Anfouchy (via Ramleh Station); the Circular Line: Karmouz–Ismail I Square–Rond Point and Ragheb Pasha–Ismail I Square.

Its power station supplied power for industrial purposes to Alexandria. It had workshops at Karmouz and Moharrem Bey. It owned shares in the Alexandria Transport and Industrial Co., an investment of L.E. 144,000 out of a total paid up capital of L.E. 150,000.

The tram system in Ramleh was also operated by the company. On January 1, 1929, the Government took over the system by administrative means and the Egyptian State Railways was entrusted with running the service. The company took action, claiming L.E. 1,200,000. On May 14, 1940, the Alexandria Mixed Court fixed the sum at L.E. 373,006 plus interest of 5% from date of assignment.

Offices: 3 Zaghloul Pasha Square, Alexandria.

Capital: £375 divided into 375,000 Ordninary shares of £1 each, fully paid.

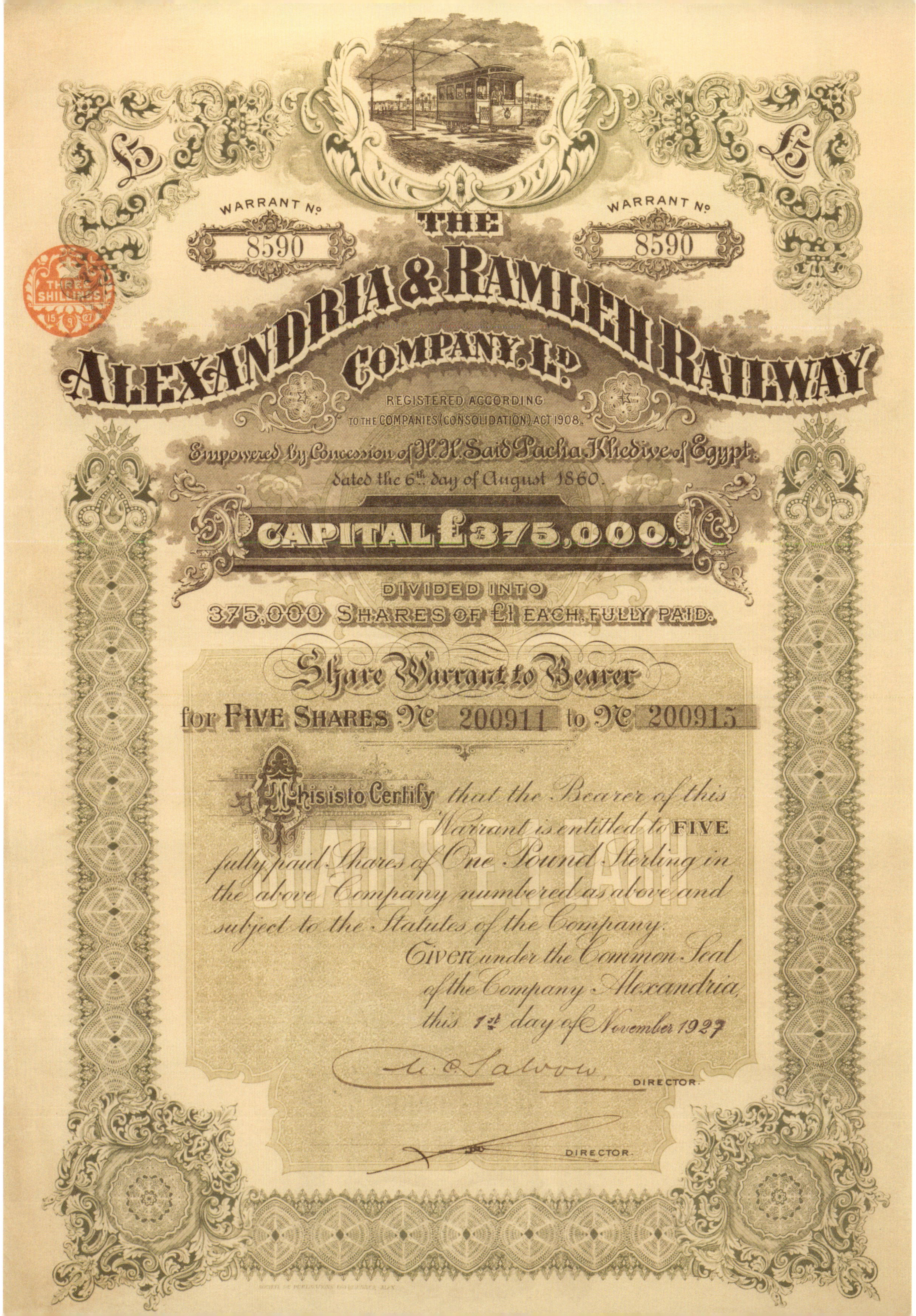

£5 £5

WARRANT No 8590

WARRANT No 8590

THREE SHILLINGS 15 9 27

THE ALEXANDRIA & RAMLEH RAILWAY COMPANY, LD

REGISTERED ACCORDING TO THE COMPANIES (CONSOLIDATION) ACT 1908.

Empowered by Concession of H. H. Said Pacha Khedive of Egypt. dated the 6th day of August 1860.

CAPITAL £375,000,

DIVIDED INTO

375,000 SHARES OF £1 EACH, FULLY PAID.

Share Warrant to Bearer

for FIVE SHARES No 200911 to No 200915

SHARES £1 EACH

This is to Certify that the Bearer of this Warrant is entitled to FIVE fully paid Shares of One Pound Sterling in the above Company numbered as above and subject to the Statutes of the Company.

Given under the Common Seal of the Company Alexandria, this 1st day of November 1927

[signature] DIRECTOR.

[signature] DIRECTOR.

Salvagos wealth and communal prestige notwithstanding, they were regarded by the community at large as ardent anglophiles. With the British protectorate in full swing, Constantine Salvagos knew on which side his toast was buttered. Having identified himself with the British, both politically and economically, Constantine Salvagos was foremost in line to be rewarded by Lord Cromer for his thoughtfulness and cooperation. The British proconsul in Cairo was amongst the first to recognize the merits of having Constantine join the founding board of that latest of British colonial banks. Just as welcoming was Raphael Suarès, for Salvagos was an old business colleague ever since they successfully founded together the Credit Foncier Bank in 1880. Perhaps, they could set another financial milestone together.

L'Union Fonciere d'Égypte

Registered in June 6, 1905 to undertake general land business. In December 31, 1945, it owned 3,660 feddans of agricultural land. The Rodah estate was acquired in November 1944 from the Daira Toussoun. Of the total area, 2,988 feddans are let to farmers at an average rent of P.T. 1,262 per feddan and 672 feddans are cultivated by the company itself.

Head Office: Immobilia Building, 26 Cherif Pasha Street, Cairo.

Capital:
£325,000 divided into 65,000 5% Cumulative Ordinary shares of £5 each, fully paid.
5,000 Founders shares of no par value entitle to 25% of surplus profits after payment of accumulated arrears of dividends on 5% Cumulative Ordinary shares.

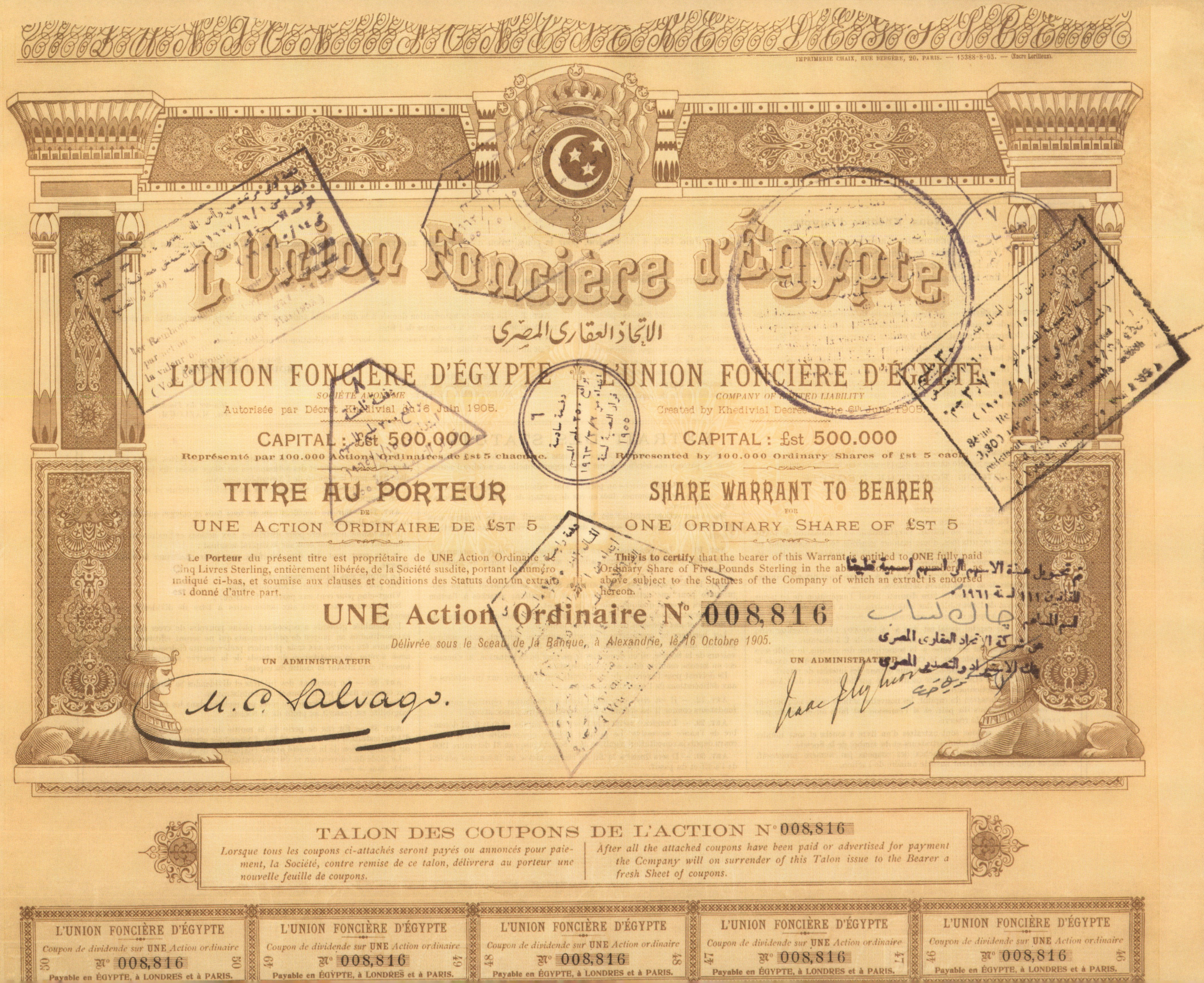

IMPRIMERIE CHAIX, RUE BERGÈRE, 20, PARIS. — 15388-8-05. — (Encre Lorilleux).

L'Union Foncière d'Égypte

الاتحاد العقاري المصري

L'UNION FONCIÈRE D'ÉGYPTE	L'UNION FONCIÈRE D'ÉGYPTE
SOCIÉTÉ ANONYME	COMPANY OF LIMITED LIABILITY
Autorisée par Décret Khédivial du 6 Juin 1905.	Created by Khedivial Decree of the 6th June 1905.
CAPITAL : £st 500.000	CAPITAL : £st 500.000
Représenté par 100.000 Actions Ordinaires de £st 5 chacune.	Represented by 100.000 Ordinary Shares of £st 5 each.
TITRE AU PORTEUR	**SHARE WARRANT TO BEARER**
DE	FOR
UNE ACTION ORDINAIRE DE £ST 5	ONE ORDINARY SHARE OF £ST 5
Le Porteur du présent titre est propriétaire de UNE Action Ordinaire de Cinq Livres Sterling, entièrement libérée, de la Société susdite, portant le numéro indiqué ci-bas, et soumise aux clauses et conditions des Statuts dont un extrait est donné d'autre part.	**This is to certify** that the bearer of this Warrant is entitled to ONE fully paid Ordinary Share of Five Pounds Sterling in the above Company numbered as above subject to the Statutes of the Company of which an extract is endorsed hereon.

UNE Action Ordinaire N° 008,816

Délivrée sous le Sceau de la Banque, à Alexandrie, le 16 Octobre 1905.

UN ADMINISTRATEUR	UN ADMINISTRATEUR
M. C. Salvago	Isaac Cattaui

الاتحاد العقاري المصري

TALON DES COUPONS DE L'ACTION N° 008,816

Lorsque tous les coupons ci-attachés seront payés ou annoncés pour paiement, la Société, contre remise de ce talon, délivrera au porteur une nouvelle feuille de coupons.

After all the attached coupons have been paid or advertised for payment the Company will on surrender of this Talon issue to the Bearer a fresh Sheet of coupons.

50	49	48	47	46
L'UNION FONCIÈRE D'ÉGYPTE	L'UNION FONCIÈRE D'ÉGYPTE	L'UNION FONCIÈRE D'ÉGYPTE	L'UNION FONCIÈRE D'ÉGYPTE	L'UNION FONCIÈRE D'ÉGYPTE
Coupon de dividende sur UNE *Action ordinaire*	*Coupon de dividende sur* UNE *Action ordinaire*	*Coupon de dividende sur* UNE *Action ordinaire*	*Coupon de dividende sur* UNE *Action ordinaire*	*Coupon de dividende sur* UNE *Action ordinaire*
N° 008,816	N° 008,816	N° 008,816	N° 008,816	N° 008,816
Payable en ÉGYPTE, à LONDRES et à PARIS.	Payable en ÉGYPTE, à LONDRES et à PARIS.	Payable en ÉGYPTE, à LONDRES et à PARIS.	Payable en ÉGYPTE, à LONDRES et à PARIS.	Payable en ÉGYPTE, à LONDRES et à PARIS.

The Credit Foncier Egyptien

Built in 1903, opposite what was once Cairo's old hippodrome, the Credit Foncier Egyptien is by far the oldest bank in Cairo. Founded in 1880, it preceded the National Bank of Egypt by 18 years.

Credit Foncier's founders and shareholders were predominantly French or French-protected until it was nationalized in the late 1950s. On the other hand, the National Bank of Egypt was run as an exclusive British club during its first forty-seven years of existence. In fact, the creation of the National Bank was in part an effort by Egypt's British occupiers to break or circumvent France's hold over the country's banking system.

It was no coincidence that the Credit Foncier chose the corner plot on Manakh (later Abdel Khalek Sarwat Pasha) Street and Emad al-Din on which to erect its imposing Cairo headquarters in 1903-4. Originally, the area had been an extension to the old hippodrome where so many races took place in the middle of the 19th century. In the 1860s, both the hippodrome and the outlying area were earmarked for urban development as part of Khedive Ismail's scheme to create the new Europeanized district of Ismailia.

An entire block of the newly traced district was picked up by two of modern Cairo's biggest land speculators: Mr. Karl Heinrich Beyerle and Mr. Raphael Menachem Suarès. Both gentlemen were founding shareholders of the Credit Foncier Egyptien, which, at the time, had its main offices in Alexandria. And both had been bankers to Khedive Ismail at one time or another. In 1873, Beyerle represented Herman Oppenheimer & Co. in Egypt — the noted financial institution that would later play a capital role in bankrupting the Khedive.

Most of the commercial property surrounding the bank's proposed Cairo branch, including the semi-circled Cercle Risotto still standing today, belonged to Suarès, hence the name Rondpoint Suarès. It was only in the early 1940s that the name of the roundabout changed to Mustafa Kamel; as though to indicate changing times, the name of the famous French-educated Ottoman-Egyptian nationalist replaced that of the wealthy Italo-Mediterranean Jewish capitalist.

Credit Foncier Egyptien

The Credit Foncier Egyptien was incorporated in Egypt by the Khedivial Decree of February 15, 1880. Its purpose was advancing loans on mortgage to city or country landowners in Egypt. It was also empowered to grant loans in Egypt to provinces, municipalities, syndicates depending on the Government and possessing special authorization, syndicates independent of Governemnt control, as well as hospitals, public establishments and companies holding concessions for public services. The loan may be with or without mortgage. The company was authorized to open current accounts on mortgage or on security and to discount values guaranteed by securities.

Head Office: 35 Malika Farida Street, Cairo.

Capital:
L.E. 3,857,500 (FF 100,000,000) divided into 400,000 Ordinary shares of FF 500 each, issued to bearer, of which FF 250 has been paid-up (Capital subscribed FF 200,000,000, or L.E. 7,715,000).
2,000 Founders shares of no nominal value, created in 1880. In 1904, these were subdivided into tenths (i.e. 20,000 parts) with a view to making them more accessible to smaller investors.

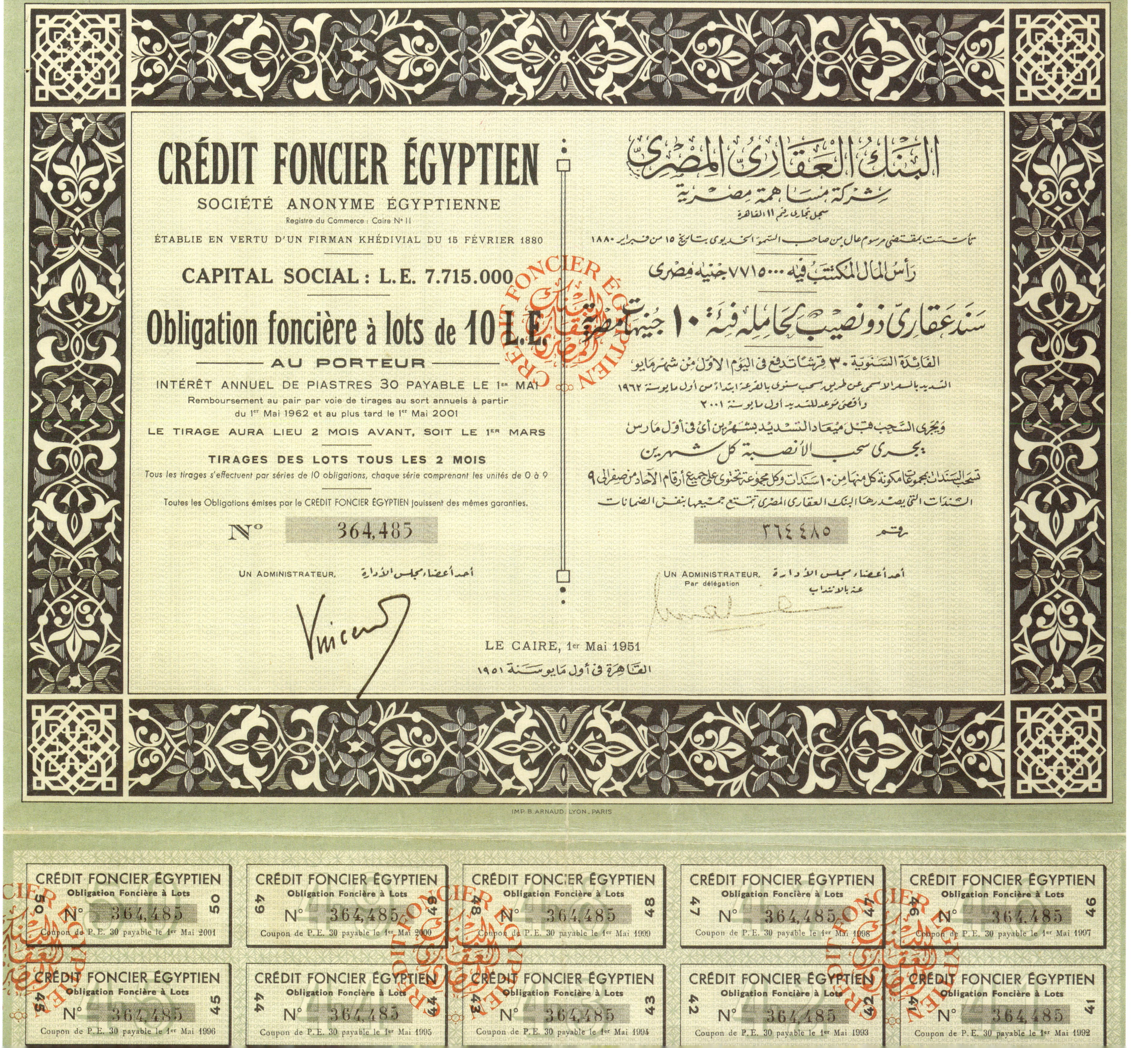

CRÉDIT FONCIER ÉGYPTIEN

SOCIÉTÉ ANONYME ÉGYPTIENNE

Registre du Commerce : Caire N° 11

ÉTABLIE EN VERTU D'UN FIRMAN KHÉDIVIAL DU 15 FÉVRIER 1880

CAPITAL SOCIAL : L.E. 7.715.000

Obligation foncière à lots de 10 L.E.

AU PORTEUR

INTÉRÊT ANNUEL DE PIASTRES 30 PAYABLE LE 1er MAI

Remboursement au pair par voie de tirages au sort annuels à partir du 1er Mai 1962 et au plus tard le 1er Mai 2001

LE TIRAGE AURA LIEU 2 MOIS AVANT, SOIT LE 1er MARS

TIRAGES DES LOTS TOUS LES 2 MOIS

Tous les tirages s'effectuent par séries de 10 obligations, chaque série comprenant les unités de 0 à 9

Toutes les Obligations émises par le CRÉDIT FONCIER ÉGYPTIEN jouissent des mêmes garanties.

N° 364,485

البنك العقارى المصرى

شركة مساهمة مصرية

سجل تجارى رقم ١١ القاهرة

تأسست بمقتضى مرسوم عال من صاحب السمو الخديوى بتاريخ ١٥ من فبراير ١٨٨٠

رأس المال المكتتب فيه ٧٧١٥٠٠٠ جنيه مصرى

سند عقارى ذو نصيب لحامله فئة ١٠ جنيهات مصرية

الفائدة السنوية ٣٠ قرشا تدفع فى اليوم الأول من شهر مايو

التسديد بالسعر الاسمى عن طريق سحب سنوى بالقرعة ابتداء من أول مايو سنة ١٩٦٢

وأقصى موعد للتسديد أول مايو سنة ٢٠٠١

ويجرى السحب قبل ميعاد التسديد بشهرين أى فى أول مارس

يجرى سحب الأنصبة كل شهرين

تسحب السندات بمجموعات مكونة كل منها من ١٠ سندات وكل مجموعة تحتوى على جميع أرقام الآحاد من صفر إلى ٩

السندات التى يصدرها البنك العقارى المصرى تتمتع جميعها بنفس الضمانات

رقم ٣٦٤٤٨٥

UN ADMINISTRATEUR, أحد أعضاء مجلس الإدارة

UN ADMINISTRATEUR, Par délégation — أحد أعضاء مجلس الإدارة عن الانتداب

LE CAIRE, 1er Mai 1951

القاهرة فى أول مايو سنة ١٩٥١

IMP. B. ARNAUD, LYON, PARIS

CRÉDIT FONCIER ÉGYPTIEN — Obligation Foncière à Lots — N° 364,485 — 50 — Coupon de P.E. 30 payable le 1er Mai 2001

CRÉDIT FONCIER ÉGYPTIEN — Obligation Foncière à Lots — N° 364,485 — 49 — Coupon de P.E. 30 payable le 1er Mai 2000

CRÉDIT FONCIER ÉGYPTIEN — Obligation Foncière à Lots — N° 364,485 — 48 — Coupon de P.E. 30 payable le 1er Mai 1999

CRÉDIT FONCIER ÉGYPTIEN — Obligation Foncière à Lots — N° 364,485 — 47 — Coupon de P.E. 30 payable le 1er Mai 1998

CRÉDIT FONCIER ÉGYPTIEN — Obligation Foncière à Lots — N° 364,485 — 46 — Coupon de P.E. 30 payable le 1er Mai 1997

CRÉDIT FONCIER ÉGYPTIEN — Obligation Foncière à Lots — N° 364,485 — 45 — Coupon de P.E. 30 payable le 1er Mai 1996

CRÉDIT FONCIER ÉGYPTIEN — Obligation Foncière à Lots — N° 364,485 — 44 — Coupon de P.E. 30 payable le 1er Mai 1995

CRÉDIT FONCIER ÉGYPTIEN — Obligation Foncière à Lots — N° 364,485 — 43 — Coupon de P.E. 30 payable le 1er Mai 1994

CRÉDIT FONCIER ÉGYPTIEN — Obligation Foncière à Lots — N° 364,485 — 42 — Coupon de P.E. 30 payable le 1er Mai 1993

CRÉDIT FONCIER ÉGYPTIEN — Obligation Foncière à Lots — N° 364,485 — 41 — Coupon de P.E. 30 payable le 1er Mai 1992

Educating the elite

It was a splendid day in Alexandria on the afternoon of 24th of May 1906, the birthday anniversary of the late Queen Victoria, a special occasion as royalty, pashas, ministers and Alexandrine notables gathered at Domaine de Siouf, a coastal retreat several kilometers east of the city. They had come to celebrate the kickoff of what would become the latest symbol of British hegemony in the region: Victoria College. The empress-queen was again being immortalized in yet another corner of the globe.

Even though Egypt was technically an Ottoman province governed by the sultan's hereditary vassal, Khedive Abbas Hilmi II, Britain had in fact taken over the reigns of power in September 1882 when it launched its military occupation, which was to last for seven decades. The country's real ruler in 1906 was one of Britain's greatest imperialists, the first Earl of Cromer formerly known to Egyptians as Sir Evelyn Baring of Barings Bros. fame.

Cromer’s presence at this landmark solemnization outside Alexandria added to the magic and excitement of the moment and no one dared not attend — Khedivial family included.

Few suspected that all along Cromer had been against advancing education in Egypt. "Al-Lord" believed that even a little learning was a dangerous thing, especially if the beneficiaries were colonized people. Nevertheless, he must have found some comfort in knowing that British hands would rock the cradle.

Speeches were the order of the day. On behalf of the Muslim community, the Arabic master, Sheik Mohammed Hamed, spoke in Arabic, while E.B. Gould, the British consul in Alexandria, made his statement in English. Also speaking from the dais were Lord Cromer and Baron Jacques Levi de Menashe. Together on the school's executive committee, the British lord and the Jewish baron epitomized the powerful Anglo-Jewish alliance that catalyzed the modernization of Egypt — the symbiotic relationship of the colonizer and the favored minority.

Cromer and Menashe referred in their speeches to the state of education in Egypt, which, save for the religious missions run by Jesuits and other Catholic orders, was deemed inadequate. Native schools, it was understood, could not substitute for a modern European edification. In the meantime, young men wanting to pursue advanced English education had limited choices: either attend the non-progressive religious schools, or travel to England. Now, with the creation of Victoria College, an English public school education was within easy reach.

The school operated then out of modest quarters in the Mazarita (corrupted from the word [Monsieur] Lazareth) district of Alexandria, overlooking the Eastern Harbor. The land on which the original school was built had been a gift from George Beeton Alderson, who purchased it at a discount from the Egyptian State paying LE 1500.

The school's founders quickly resolved to change the original name "British School" to "Victoria College" — the new name had a better ring and would be more conducive to fund raising both in Alexandria and England.

The school's executive committee was made up of leading Alexandrines that invariably meant a mixture of

Tramways d'Alexandrie

The Tramways d’Alexandrie was registered in Belgium on December 4, 1897. The company controls the Alexandria and Ramleh Railway Co. Ltd. in which it holds £315,860 £1 shares out of a total capital of £375,000.

The Alexandria and Ramleh Railway Co. Ltd. owned a concession from the Alexandria Municipality for running electric tramways in the city of Alexandria. The 50-year concession expired on March 31, 1946 and was not renewed. The company had other activities outside the concession. These included workshops at Karmouz, Alexandria where mechanical constructions were undertaken. Power was also supplied for industrial purposes to the city of Alexandria with the exception of Ramleh.

Head Office: 3 Zaghloul Pasha Square, Alexandria.

Capital:
L.E. 306,660 representing the value of 12,660 Preference shares redeemed and converted into a similar number of Jouissance shares of no specified value.
33,300 Dividend (deferred) shares of no par value.

TRAMWAYS D'ALEXANDRIE (Égypte)

SOCIÉTÉ ANONYME

Constituée par acte authentique passé devant Mes ECTORS et VAN HALTEREN, notaires à Bruxelles, le 4 décembre 1897 publié au « Moniteur belge » le 23 décembre 1897

SIÈGE SOCIAL A BRUXELLES

Action Privilégiée de Cent francs au Porteur

Nº 26,835

ENTIÈREMENT LIBÉRÉE

Un Administrateur, Un Administrateur,

La feuille de coupons ci-contre étant épuisée, il en sera délivré une autre au porteur du présent titre.

Le capital social a été porté de frs 3.000.000 à frs 6.000.000 par l'émission de 30.000 actions privilégiées nouvelles de 100 frs chacune suivant acte authentique par devant Mes Ectors et Van Halteren notaires à Bruxelles, en date du 7 Mai 1898 et ce conformément à l'art. 5 des statuts.

(Publié au) Moniteur Belge du 15 Mai 1898

TITRE REMBOURSÉ ET CONVERTI EN ACTION DE JOUISSANCE CONFORMÉMENT A L'ARTICLE 38 DES STATUTS

Soc. An. des TRAMWAYS d'ALEXANDRIE (EN LIQUIDATION) 15 Mai 1951

Nº 36174. — BRUXELLES. — TYP. ET LITH. E. GUYOT, RUE PACHÉCO, 12.

Europeans and Levantine Jews, plus the city's senior civil servants most of whom were British.

The first president of the executive committee was Sir Charles Cookson, British consul general in Alexandria. When he died before the completion of the new Victoria College, he was automatically replaced by E.B. Gould.

By agreement, the chief British representative (pro-consul, later high commissioner and ambassador) to Egypt, the consul general in Alexandria and the president of the British Chamber of Commerce of Egypt were the school's ex-officio trustees.

One of Alexandria's noted Anglo-Egyptians, Charles R. Lias, a graduate of Marlborough College and King's College, Cambridge, became Victoria College's first headmaster, receiving 500 pounds per annum.

If in 1902-3 there were only 45 students enrolled, by 1906 they had increased more than threefold to 186. They included 13 nationalities broken down into three religious groups; there were 80 Christians, 67 Jews and 39 Muslims, mirroring the city's upper-class mosaic. The school's motto was *Cuncti gens una sumus*, meaning "joined together as one people".

With high demand for enrollment, it was evident that newer and bigger premises were needed, even though there were already plans to enlarge the old ones. Even before the move, an entire new floor was added courtesy of contractor Kevork Meramedjian under the supervision of McClure & Dorling, who had built the original building conforming to architect H. Favarger original design.

The new 17-acre grounds at Domaine de Siouf were mostly bought with private donations. The Khedive donated part of the land. With space no longer a major consideration, the new school was conceived to accommodate upwards of 500 students.

The only other edifice worth mentioning in the immediate area was Saray al Hazina (Palace of Sorrows) which belonged to the Khediva-Mother. The hilltop saray was the Khedive's temporary residence while he supervised the construction of his seaside palais de chasse, Montaza Palace.

In time for the groundbreaking ceremony, the Bacos & Schutz tramlines which had heretofore ended at San Stefano, were extended further east. The new terminus was situated midway between Saray al Hazina station and the school's new grounds, not too far from the Alexandria–Abou Kir–Rosetta Railway.

Within site of the new Victoria College was another famous landmark, the Ramleh Casino. This fin-de-siecle monument constructed in 1886-7 was imagined and conceived by Boghos Nubar Pasha, son of the Armenian statesman-administrator Nubar Nubarian. Having studied at the École Central in Paris, Boghos was infatuated with the famous casinos and seaside resorts dotting the Franco-Belgian coast between the fashionable towns of Deauville and Ostende. The result was Ramleh-Les-Bains' majestic San Stefano Hotel & Casino.

The casino, the saray and the new English public school could be reached by motor coach via Strada Rossa

Société des Autobus d'Alexandrie

The Société des Autobus d'Alexandrie was registered on September 6, 1932 to operate bus services. The company owned a concession from the Alexandria Municipality to run motor-bus services between Alexandria and the suburb of Ramleh. The concession expired on December 31, 1937 and was not renewed. In 1942 the company was reorganized and lorry service for the transport of goods between Alexandria and other points in Egypt was inaugurated.

Office and Garage: 2 Cimarosa Street (Sidi Gaber), Ramleh, Alexandria.

Capital:
L.E. 25,000 divided into 6,250 Ordinary shares of L.E. 4 each, fully paid.

شركة سيارات اتوبوس اسكندرية

شركة مساهمة مصرية

SOCIÉTÉ DES AUTOBUS D'ALEXANDRIE

SOCIÉTÉ ANONYME EGYPTIENNE

AUTORISÉE PAR DÉCRET ROYAL EN DATE DU 6 SEPTEMBRE 1932

SIÈGE SOCIAL: ALEXANDRIE, EGYPTE

5 ACTIONS

100 L.EG.

Capital réduit à L.Eg. 5000.- par suite du remboursement de L.Eg. 16.- par action, effectué suivant décision de l'Assemblée Générale Extraordinaire du 30 Avril 1947.

CAPITAL SOCIAL ENTIÈREMENT VERSÉ L.EG. 25.000

DIVISÉ EN 1250 ACTIONS DE L.EG. 20 CHACUNE

ENTIÈREMENT LIBÉRÉES

CINQ ACTIONS AU PORTEUR

DE LIVRES EGYPTIENNES VINGT CHACUNE

UN ADMINISTRATEUR

UN ADMINISTRATEUR

Nº 0376 à Nº 0380

Alexandrie, Mai 1947.

LITH Fres VENTURA-ALEXANDRIE

SOCIÉTÉ DES AUTOBUS D'ALEXANDRIE
SOCIÉTÉ ANONYME EGYPTIENNE
50 CINQ ACTIONS 50
Nº 0376 à Nº 0380
COUPON PAYABLE AU PORTEUR

SOCIÉTÉ DES AUTOBUS D'ALEXANDRIE
SOCIÉTÉ ANONYME EGYPTIENNE
49 CINQ ACTIONS 49
Nº 0376 à Nº 0380
COUPON PAYABLE AU PORTEUR

SOCIÉTÉ DES AUTOBUS D'ALEXANDRIE
SOCIÉTÉ ANONYME EGYPTIENNE
48 CINQ ACTIONS 48
Nº 0376 à Nº 0380
COUPON PAYABLE AU PORTEUR

SOCIÉTÉ DES AUTOBUS D'ALEXANDRIE
SOCIÉTÉ ANONYME EGYPTIENNE
47 CINQ ACTIONS 47
Nº 0376 à Nº 0380
COUPON PAYABLE AU PORTEUR

SOCIÉTÉ DES AUTOBUS D'ALEXANDRIE
SOCIÉTÉ ANONYME EGYPTIENNE
46 CINQ ACTIONS 46
Nº 0376 à Nº 0380
COUPON PAYABLE AU PORTEUR

SOCIÉTÉ DES AUTOBUS D'ALEXANDRIE
SOCIÉTÉ ANONYME EGYPTIENNE
45 CINQ ACTIONS 45
Nº 0376 à Nº 0380
COUPON PAYABLE AU PORTEUR

SOCIÉTÉ DES AUTOBUS D'ALEXANDRIE
SOCIÉTÉ ANONYME EGYPTIENNE
44 CINQ ACTIONS 44
Nº 0376 à Nº 0380
COUPON PAYABLE AU PORTEUR

SOCIÉTÉ DES AUTOBUS D'ALEXANDRIE
SOCIÉTÉ ANONYME EGYPTIENNE
43 CINQ ACTIONS 43
Nº 0376 à Nº 0380
COUPON PAYABLE AU PORTEUR

SOCIÉTÉ DES AUTOBUS D'ALEXANDRIE
SOCIÉTÉ ANONYME EGYPTIENNE
42 CINQ ACTIONS 42
Nº 0376 à Nº 0380
COUPON PAYABLE AU PORTEUR

SOCIÉTÉ DES AUTOBUS D'ALEXANDRIE
SOCIÉTÉ ANONYME EGYPTIENNE
41 CINQ ACTIONS 41
Nº 0376 à Nº 0380
COUPON PAYABLE AU PORTEUR

(afterwards Fouad Avenue, now Tarik al Horeya). Ramleh's main artery ran a west-east axis from Alexandria's Rue Porte de Rosette through various residential townships until it finished at Siouf. Strada Rossa, or Red Street, was so named because it was covered with reddish potsherds from the ruins of Roman Alexandria. The Corniche was still unheard of.

"Ramleh" comes from the Arabic word for sand, and that's exactly how Alexandria's cosmopolitan set perceived this narrow, sparsely Bedouin-inhabited bayside stretch sandwiched between the Mediterranean to the north and salty marshes to the south. Ramleh's convenient location and the steady northerly winds sweeping across its rows of palm-decked dunes had a seductive effect on Alexandria's taipans and compradores, and it was thanks to a gathering of these far-sighted entrepreneurs that in 1860 the decision was made to link Ramleh with Alexandria by rail.

Soon after, Constantin Zervudachi, E. Cornish, Constantine and P. Salvagos, Charles Royle, Dr. Varenhorst Pasha and A. Caillard founded the Alexandria & Ramleh Railway Co., with a concession of 70 years. Just into the twentieth century, the company replaced the steam engine with electrification.

By the summer of 1890, a regular train service ran between Alexandria and San Stefano, peaking at 24 trains per day. On Sundays, the 5,048 chairs belonging to the seaside casino could barely cope with the influx of weekend visitors. The waiting list to join the genteel San Stefano Club was twice as long as its 425 membership.

As Ramleh became increasingly accessible, the Casino's owners decided to act in response to these welcome statistics — in 1893, Nicolas Sabagh, the casino's Syrian secretary, commissioned architect Leon Stienon of the Alexandria Municipality and part-time Dutch consul-general, to add a new a western wing.

The enlarged hotel was run by Alexandria's maverick hotelier Luigi Steinschneider, who later became the director of Zamalek's Gezira Palace Hotel, when it was still managed by the Egyptian branch of the Wagons-Lits.

Back in Ramleh, another European, Jules Castravelli, ran the important tramway station of San Stefano. His opposite number at the Alexandria terminal situated at Rue al-Chatby (also known as Ramleh Station) was Signor Marsiglio.

By 1910, Ramleh's various suburbs had matured into small townships. Each had a distinct flavor and its own set of notables, their houses surrounded by vast gardens. With the use of cisterns for storing pumped water from the Mahmoudia fresh-water canal south of Bulkley, the once-empty sands flowered. These topographical transformations were amply visible from the trams' windows. Alexandrines marveled at the horticultural wonders created by their city's business elite. Equally breathtaking were the grand homes belonging to Alexandria's colonial merchants, money-lenders, and its cotton, tobacco and timber barons.

At Bacos, the gardens of Tousson Pasha, Camilleri and Sinadino-Ralli exuded year-round colors and fragrances. It was the same at Seffer, with the garden-plantations of Prince Hussein Kamel, Contandinidis and Tachau. Passing

Société Anonyme des Drogueries d'Égypte

Registered on April 6, 1914 to operate as wholesale and retail chemists with nine retail drug stores, of which six are in Cairo, two in Alexandria, and one in Port Said. The company was controlled and financed by the Société d'Avances Commerciales.

Head Office: 12, Mahdi Street, Ezbekia, Cairo.

Capital:
L.E. 75,000 divided into 18,75 Ordinary shares of L.E. 4 each fully paid.

1 ACTION

1 ACTION

SOCIÉTÉ ANONYME DES DROGUERIES D'EGYPTE

Société Anonyme Egyptienne

AUTORISÉE PAR DÉCRET KHÉDIVIAL DU 6 AVRIL 1914 PUBLIÉ AU JOURNAL OFFICIEL DU 18 AVRIL 1914.

CAPITAL SOCIAL L.E. 75.000

DIVISÉ EN 18.750 ACTIONS AU PORTEUR DE LIVRES EGYPTIENNES QUATRE CHACUNE.

suivant décision de l'Assemblée générale des Actionnaires du 18 Décembre 1943

Siége Social : Le Caire

formément aux Résolutions de
mblée Générale Extraordinaire
Décembre 1951,
Le Capital social est fixé à L.E.
présenté par 25.125 actions de
chacune, entièrement libérées

UNE ACTION AU PORTEUR

DE LIVRES EGYPTIENNES QUATRE

ENTIÈREMENT LIBÉRÉE

UN ADMINISTRATEUR

Nº 12620

UN ADMINISTRATEUR

Le Caire, le 5 Janvier 1944

R.C. Nº 10866

L.E. 4

S D E A

L.E. 4

WHITEHEAD MORRIS (EGYPT) LIMITED

SOCIÉTÉ ANONYME DES DROGUERIES D'EGYPTE UNE ACTION au PORTEUR Nº 12620 COUPON DE DIVIDENDE AU PORTEUR PAYABLE AU SIÈGE DE LA SOCIÉTÉ AU CAIRE 50	SOCIÉTÉ ANONYME DES DROGUERIES D'EGYPTE UNE ACTION au PORTEUR Nº 12620 COUPON DE DIVIDENDE AU PORTEUR PAYABLE AU SIÈGE DE LA SOCIÉTÉ AU CAIRE 49	SOCIÉTÉ ANONYME DES DROGUERIES D'EGYPTE UNE ACTION au PORTEUR Nº 12620 COUPON DE DIVIDENDE AU PORTEUR PAYABLE AU SIÈGE DE LA SOCIÉTÉ AU CAIRE 48	SOCIÉTÉ ANONYME DES DROGUERIES D'EGYPTE UNE ACTION au PORTEUR Nº 12620 COUPON DE DIVIDENDE AU PORTEUR PAYABLE AU SIÈGE DE LA SOCIÉTÉ AU CAIRE 47	SOCIÉTÉ ANONYME DES DROGUERIES D'EGYPTE UNE ACTION au PORTEUR Nº 12620 COUPON DE DIVIDENDE AU PORTEUR PAYABLE AU SIÈGE DE LA SOCIÉTÉ AU CAIRE 46
SOCIÉTÉ ANONYME DES DROGUERIES D'EGYPTE UNE ACTION au PORTEUR Nº 12620 COUPON DE DIVIDENDE AU PORTEUR PAYABLE AU SIÈGE DE LA SOCIÉTÉ AU CAIRE 45	SOCIÉTÉ ANONYME DES DROGUERIES D'EGYPTE UNE ACTION au PORTEUR Nº 12620 COUPON DE DIVIDENDE AU PORTEUR PAYABLE AU SIÈGE DE LA SOCIÉTÉ AU CAIRE 44	SOCIÉTÉ ANONYME DES DROGUERIES D'EGYPTE UNE ACTION au PORTEUR Nº 12620 COUPON DE DIVIDENDE AU PORTEUR PAYABLE AU SIÈGE DE LA SOCIÉTÉ AU CAIRE 43	SOCIÉTÉ ANONYME DES DROGUERIES D'EGYPTE UNE ACTION au PORTEUR Nº 12620 COUPON DE DIVIDENDE AU PORTEUR PAYABLE AU SIÈGE DE LA SOCIÉTÉ AU CAIRE 42	SOCIÉTÉ ANONYME DES DROGUERIES D'EGYPTE UNE ACTION au PORTEUR Nº 12620 COUPON DE DIVIDENDE AU PORTEUR PAYABLE AU SIÈGE DE LA SOCIÉTÉ AU CAIRE 41

through Zizinia station, tram riders gawked at the palatial home of Count Macandro Zizinia.

In Schutz and beyond, the villas of Zervudachi, Zancarol, Dikeos, Sursock and Cattaui dominated the scene. In an era where drip irrigation was as remote as Mars, the springtime horticulture show at Casino San Stefano was kept alive for over half a century.

Along the scenic tramway, it was obvious that Alexandria's diverse foreign communities had already staked their claims in Ramleh. Villa Allen, Villa Hicks, Villa Peak, Villa Kingham, (Sir George) Alderson Castle, Sidney Carver House and Moss Hill were obviously British. Villa Augusto Luzatto and Villa Emanuel Stross belonged to nationals from quaint and unpronounceable Austro-Hungarian dominions. Meanwhile, Villa Princess and Villa Reale belonged to minor nobility from Ruritania-like principalities and wealthy traders who aspired to a papal coat of arms, like the Zoghebs and the Debanes.

Other Levantines include the owners of Villa Karam (ex-Tamvaco), Villa Marelli, Palais Joseph Pharaon, Villa Spanopoulo, Villa Maestracci and Villa Benachi. There was also Villa Hermitage, belonging to Monsieur Laurens, the French tobacco dealer. Like Mr. Fleming, he had an entire garden district named after him. Another district was named after Perikles Glymonopoulo, director of the Alexandria and Ramleh Railway Company.

Mr. Glymonopoulo was also the administrator of the Egyptian Trust and Investment Company that owned large land holdings in the district of Ramleh. He was among the first to realize that it was evident additional tram line branches would be required to service the sprawling new suburbs east of Alexandria.

"What's this name?" Ilya Perrera exclaimed, pointing his small hand in the direction of a house not too far from the tram tracks. "It doesn't sound like they're from these parts," replied his older school chum Alexander Ruppa. On their way to Victoria, their curiosity was piqued by a sign on a garden gate that said "Villa Abaza".

On ordinary school days, one would run into all kinds of rowdy students, identifiable by their different uniforms. At each station some got off. At Bacos was L'Ecole des Freres, and at Fleming was the famous Notre Dame de Sion.

Last to alight were Perrera and Ruppa along with their schoolmates Fianni, Nadler, Levy, Coroneos and Vitsentzos. Like any public school in England, they sported flannel caps, gray shorts and striped school ties — probably purchased at one of Alexandria's two famous Welsh-owned department stores, Davies Bryan and Robert Hughes Outfitters. On their blazers, Perrera and Ruppa proudly wore the VC badge. This was sometimes flanked with golden leaves, denoting the bearer as a monitor or a prefect. The head boy had the most leaves, with the initials "HB" appended.

As Egypt's first generation of future "Old Boys" arrived at their destination, the Ramleh tramway reached the end of the line.

The General Warehouses of Egypt

Registered on December 15, 1943 to build storage plants in the customs zone of Alexandria and other ports capable of storing perishable goods at correct temperatures. In addition, general warehouses were to be build in the city. Advances against goods were also be effected. The company also acted as transport contractors, as well as shipping, clearing and forwarding agent.

Head Office: 22 Salah el-Din Street, Alexandria.

Capital:
L.E. 150,000 divided into 37,500 Ordinary shares of L.E. 4 each, fully paid.

25 ACTIONS

25 ACTIONS

المستودعات المصرية العامة

شركة مساهمة مصرية

THE GENERAL WAREHOUSES OF EGYPT

SOCIÉTÉ ANONYME EGYPTIENNE

Autorisée par Decret Royal du 15 Décembre 1943

Reg du Comm. Alex Nº 27563

Siège Social:

ALEXANDRIE (Egypte)

CAPITAL AUTORISÉ L.E. 150.000

DIVISÉ EN 37.500 ACTIONS DE L.E. 4 CHACUNE

TITRE AU PORTEUR DE

VINGT-CINQ ACTIONS

ENTIÈREMENT LIBÉRÉES

المرخص بها بمرسوم ملكي بتاريخ ١٥ ديسمبر سنة ١٩٤٣

السجل التجاري رقم ٢٧٥٦٣ الاسكندرية

المركز الرئيسي بالاسكندرية

رأس المال : ١٥٠٫٠٠٠ جنيه مصري

موزع على ٣٧٥٠٠ سهم قيمة كل سهم منها اربعة جنيهات مصرية

سند لحامله

بقيمة خمسة وعشرون سهما وقيمة كل سهم أربعة جنيهات مصرية

مسددة بالكامل

Capital porté de L.E. 100.000 à L.E. 150.000
Décision de l'Assemblée Générale Extraordinaire du 6 Août 1946

Capital porté à L.E. 200.000
Décision de l'Assemblée Générale Extraordinaire du 14 Décembre 1946

Nº 36901 À Nº 36925

رفع رأس المال من ١٠٠٫٠٠٠ جنيه الى ١٥٠٫٠٠٠ جنيه
قرار الجمعية العمومية الغير عادية بتاريخ ٦ أغسطس سنة ١٩٤٦

رفع رأس المال الى ٢٠٠٫٠٠٠ جنيه
قرار الجمعية العمومية الغير عادية بتاريخ ١٤ ديسمبر سنة ١٩٤٦

Alexandrie, le FEV 1947 الاسكندرية في

عضو مجلس الادارة

UN ADMINISTRATEUR

عضو مجلس الادارة

UN ADMINISTRATEUR

THE GENERAL WAREHOUSES OF EGYPT SOCIÉTÉ ANONYME EGYPTIENNE 50 VINGT-CINQ ACTIONS 50 Nº 36901 À Nº 36925 COUPON PAYABLE AU PORTEUR	THE GENERAL WAREHOUSES OF EGYPT SOCIÉTÉ ANONYME EGYPTIENNE 49 VINGT-CINQ ACTIONS 49 Nº 36901 À Nº 36925 COUPON PAYABLE AU PORTEUR	THE GENERAL WAREHOUSES OF EGYPT SOCIÉTÉ ANONYME EGYPTIENNE 48 VINGT-CINQ ACTIONS 48 Nº 36901 À Nº 36925 COUPON PAYABLE AU PORTEUR	THE GENERAL WAREHOUSES OF EGYPT SOCIÉTÉ ANONYME EGYPTIENNE 47 VINGT-CINQ ACTIONS 47 Nº 36901 À Nº 36925 COUPON PAYABLE AU PORTEUR	THE GENERAL WAREHOUSES OF EGYPT SOCIÉTÉ ANONYME EGYPTIENNE 46 VINGT-CINQ ACTIONS 46 Nº 36901 À Nº 36925 COUPON PAYABLE AU PORTEUR
THE GENERAL WAREHOUSES OF EGYPT SOCIÉTÉ ANONYME EGYPTIENNE 45 VINGT-CINQ ACTIONS 45 Nº 36901 À Nº 36925 COUPON PAYABLE AU PORTEUR	THE GENERAL WAREHOUSES OF EGYPT SOCIÉTÉ ANONYME EGYPTIENNE 44 VINGT-CINQ ACTIONS 44 Nº 36901 À Nº 36925 COUPON PAYABLE AU PORTEUR	THE GENERAL WAREHOUSES OF EGYPT SOCIÉTÉ ANONYME EGYPTIENNE 43 VINGT-CINQ ACTIONS 43 Nº 36901 À Nº 36925 COUPON PAYABLE AU PORTEUR	THE GENERAL WAREHOUSES OF EGYPT SOCIÉTÉ ANONYME EGYPTIENNE 42 VINGT-CINQ ACTIONS 42 Nº 36901 À Nº 36925 COUPON PAYABLE AU PORTEUR	THE GENERAL WAREHOUSES OF EGYPT SOCIÉTÉ ANONYME EGYPTIENNE 41 VINGT-CINQ ACTIONS 41 Nº 36901 À Nº 36925 COUPON PAYABLE AU PORTEUR
THE GENERAL WAREHOUSES OF EGYPT	THE GENERAL WAREHOUSES OF EGYPT	THE GENERAL WAREHOUSES OF EGYPT	THE GENERAL WAREHOUSES OF EGYPT	THE GENERAL WAREHOUSES OF EGYPT

When Maadi nearly replaced Heliopolis

The developers of Heliopolis were a consortium of Belgian developers led by Monsieur Edouard Empain who later became world-famous as the industrial and financial mogul "General-Baron Empain". The Egyptian partner in this vanguard turn-of-the-century venture was Boghos Nubar Pasha, son of the late Armenian prime minister of Egypt, Nubar Nubarian.

Armed with Boghos Pasha's personal entrées in the Khedivial Court, Empain was assured an equitable deal for the launch of his dream city. Yet hardly anyone knows that at the turn of the twentieth century, the Empain Group had originally considered an area south of Cairo as the site for their future city.

Even before he launched Heliopolis, Monsieur Empain had made a name for himself in Egypt when he introduced in Cairo Africa's first electrical tramway cars. Now, to achieve his other urban dream, he urgently needed to acquire an appropriate stretch of land with unlimited potential for development.

Since expanding east and west of the city were off bounds in 1900 — the Mokattam Hills to the east and the Nile to the west acting as natural barriers — the choice of land for the new city was limited to either south or north of the city where vast expanses of desert stretched ad infinitum.

One thing the Baron knew for certain: whichever place his new city was going to rise in, to ensure its success, it had to be linked to the center of Cairo by a fast and reliable railway line. In 1904, motorcars and highways were not yet popular.

To the south, a mostly empty area stood midway between Cairo and the fashionable township of Helwan-les-Bains. Due to the latter's miraculous thermal healing powers and excellent dry climate, it had become a popular winter resort frequented by pashas and beys as well as the titled members of the international café society. Khedive Mohammed Tewfik had made Helwan his principle lieu de séjour. After he died in 1892, his palace was almost immediately turned into the elegant Tewfik Palace Hotel, such was the demand for additional hotel rooms.

In 1904, Monsieur Empain realized that in order to push through his plans with a new city south of Cairo, he had to control the railway line that ran southwards from Bab el-Louk to Helwan. Failing to acquire the line would mean he would have to settle for the desert area northeast of Abassia, a considerable distance from the Nile. And he would have to create his own railway link.

With the Cairo–Helwan railway line up for sale, it was for Empain to make his move.

The railway link to Helwan was into its second decade of operation. Originally a military line running from the Citadel to a *fetishkhana* or gunpowder factory located near the river port town of Torah, it was turned over by Khedivial decree to the powerful Suarès-led financial consortium on 30 April 1888.

Realizing the railway's potential, the Suarès consortium embarked on a complete overhaul by adding a new

The Cairo Electric Railways & Heliopolis Oases Company

Registered on February 14, 1906 to acquire from the Egyptian Government a 7-year conession granting the right to build electric railways between Cairo and adjacent districts.

In 1941, the company operated the following services:
1. Cairo (Emad el-Din) to Heliopolis (Ave. Ismailia);
2. Heliopolis (San Stefano) to Abbassia;
3. Heliopolis (Almaza) to Palais-de Koubbeh.

The agreement also included the purchase of 5,952 feddans (acres) in the Abbassia desert near Cairo (later increased to 11,902 feddans) for the company to reclaim and build a new town (Heliopolis) with the amenities of a modern city.

Associated Companies:
Société Anonyme des Tramways du Caire
The Egyptian General Omnibus Co.
Société Egyptienne d'Electricite'
The African Enterprise and Development Co.

Head Office: 28 Boulevard Abbas, Heliopolis

Capital:
L.E. 2,030,009 divided into 210,500 capital shares of E.F 250 each, fully paid.
60,000 Dividend (Founders) shares of no par value.

1

The Cairo Electric Railways and Heliopolis Oases Company

Société Anonyme

Constituée le 23 Janvier 1906 et autorisée par décret Khédivial du 14 Février 1906 publié au "Journal Officiel" du Gouvernement Egyptien le 24 Février 1906

Registered 23rd January 1906 and authorized by decree of H.H the Khedive on 14th February 1906 published in the "Journal Officiel" of the Egyptian Government on 24th February 1906

SIÈGE SOCIAL: LE CAIRE

CAPITAL: 15,000,000 DE FRANCS

REPRÉSENTÉ PAR 60.000 ACTIONS DE CAPITAL DE 250 FRANCS CHACUNE ET 60.000 ACTIONS DE DIVIDENDE SANS DÉSIGNATION DE VALEUR

IN 60.000 ORDINARY SHARES OF 250 FRANCS EACH AND 60.000 FOUNDERS SHARES WITHOUT INDICATION OF VALUE

CAPITAL porté à 30 MILLIONS de francs. Par décision du Conseil d'administration du 26 Novembre 1906 prise en exécution de l'Art. 8 des statuts.

TITRE AU PORTEUR DE 1 ACTION DE CAPITAL DE 250 FRANCS

SHARE WARRANT TO BEARER FOR 1 ORDINARY SHARE OF 250 FRANCS

NUMÉRO DU TITRE 14239 SHARE WARRANT NUMBER

Nous Certifions que le porteur du présent titre est propriétaire de **UNE** *action de capital entièrement libérée de* THE CAIRO ELECTRIC RAILWAYS AND HELIOPOLIS OASES COMPANY (SOCIÉTÉ ANONYME) *portant le numéro indiqué ci-dessus et soumise aux stipulations des statuts de la Compagnie et aux résolutions des assemblées générales.*

15 MARS 1906.

This is to Certify that the bearer of this warrant is the proprietor of **ONE** *fully paid up ordinary share numbered as above in the capital of* THE CAIRO ELECTRIC RAILWAYS AND HELIOPOLIS OASES COMPANY (SOCIÉTÉ ANONYME) *subject to the articles of association of the Company and to the resolutions of the general meetings of the Company.*

15 DAY OF MARCH 1906.

Action de Jouissance

Article 28 des statuts

ADMINISTRATEURS.

1

double track route running from the Bab el-Louk district in Cairo to the Torah Town junction. The new scenic route replaced the older one, which ran from the foot of the Citadel at Midan Salah al-Din, going mostly through the desert passing alongside Bassatine and Wadi Digla before reaching Torah. From Torah to Helwan it was a straight run southwards through the quarries and agricultural fields that bordered the Nile.

The consortium also imported new rolling stock and built new stations. It was not surprising that the Cairo–Helwan railway was known in those days as the Suarès Line or *Khat Sawares* rather than by its much longer official name of The Cairo Metropolitan and Helwan Railway Company. With much fanfare, the new Bab el-Louk–Helwan line was inaugurated by Mr. Felix Suarès in November 1889.

Fifteen years later, the line was up for sale. The two bidders were Monsieur Empain's Franco-Belgian Group and the Judeo-British-owned Delta Light Railways Company.

Instead of a straight cash offer on the table, as the Belgians had done, the British-run Delta Light Railways proposed a merger with the Cairo Metropolitan Co. entailing a pro rata share swap between the shareholders. Delta Light Railways knew that its traded shares were still attractive on the London Bourse. Moreover, the company already owned and operated a narrow-gauge railway crisscrossing the Delta. Its track record was second to none.

Although it started as a freight service carrying cash crops and raw cotton from rural distribution centers to the port of Alexandria, Delta Light Railways had greatly expanded its activities. Under the chairmanship of Sir Elwin Palmer (1852-1906), a former Financial Advisor to the Government of Egypt and Governor of the National Bank, the company had set up nine days earlier the Egyptian Delta Land & Investment Company with the intention of exploiting and developing areas bordering its railway tracks "or any proposed or contemplated extension thereof".

Aside from Sir Elwin, Delta Light Railways' board of directors included Baron Jacques de Menashe and Moise Cattaui Bey. Both businessmen were related by marriage to Mr. Felix Suarès, the de facto head of the Suarès consortium. It was also well known that Monsieur Suarès was a friend and associate of Empain's European nemesis and rival, Sir Ernest Cassel.

On 29 April 1904 at 16:00, the directors of the Cairo Metropolitan and Helwan Railway Co. convened at the company's Cairo offices for an extraordinary meeting chaired by Mr. Felix Suarès. At the meeting, company secretary Monsieur Cesar Adda proceeded to read out two proposals: a merger with Delta Light Railways or the purchase of controlling shares by Empain's Société Anonyme des Tramways du Caire (a subsidiary of Société Général des Chemins de Fer Economiques).

These two very important offers were followed closely by the Cairo, Paris and London bourses. It was clear that the Metropolitan Company was either going to sell out to the Belgo-Gallic with their Syro-Levantine-Armenian proxies, or would ally itself with the Anglo-Saxon with their Jewish surrogates. Whatever the outcome, the result would have far reaching implications on Egypt's trade and economy.

Egyptian Delta Land & Investment Company

Registered in England on April 20, 1904 to carry out general real estate business, particularly the Garden City development (later known as Maadi) near Cairo.

The company's property:
–Desert land and agricultural land (including land occupied by the Sporting Club): 613 feddans;
–Agricultural Nile-front land: 198 feddans;
–Building sites for sale: 765,586 sq metres;
–Area occupied by buildings belonging to the company: 42,678 sq. metres;
–Area of roads to amortise: 422,683 sq metres;
–Old Cairo: 8,516 sq metres;
–Moulins Francais: 500 sq metres.

Head Office: 57 Road 7, Maadi, near Cairo.

Capital:
£500,000 divided into 500,000 Ordinary shares of £1 each, fully paid. Of these 333,250 are bearer shares and 166,750 are registered shares.

SHARE WARRANT

Warrant No. 34433

Nominal Value £25

SEVEN SHILLINGS & SIX PENCE

THE

Egyptian Delta Land and Investment Company,

LIMITED.

REGISTERED UNDER THE COMPANIES ACTS 1862 TO 1900.

25 SHARES

£25

Capital £ ~~250,000~~, 500,000,

DIVIDED INTO ~~250,000~~ 500,000 SHARES OF £1 EACH.

WARRANT TO BEARER FOR FULLY PAID SHARES.

This is to Certify that the bearer of this Warrant is entitled to TWENTY-FIVE fully paid up Shares of One Pound each in the above named Company numbered 205826 to 205850 inclusive subject to the regulations of the Company and to the conditions endorsed hereon.

Given under the Seal of the Company this 12 day of JUNE 1907

DIRECTOR.

SECRETARY.

"Those in favor of Delta Light Railways," called out Cesar Adda.

The shareholders hardly hesitated. Blood ran thicker than water. Debate was almost non-existent, the decision having been made even before this extraordinary meeting. Almost in chorus, the gathering declared itself unanimously in favor of a merger with the Egyptian Delta Light Railways Company.

Monsieur Empain never stood a chance.

The resolution to merge the Metropolitan Line with Delta Light Railways would unwittingly account for Maadi's definite Anglo-Saxon flavor. Had the voting gone in favor of the Société Anonyme des Tramways du Caire, Maadi might well have been built along Hindu-Saracenic lines. Monsieur Empain would now have to look north of Cairo for the founding of his dream city.

Edouard Empain's Cairo Electric Railways & Heliopolis Oases Company was duly registered in Cairo on 23 January 1906. He commenced the construction of Heliopolis the same year.

The development of Maadi by the Egyptian Delta Land & Investment Company started one year later.

Société Générale d' Electricté et de Mécanique

Registered on May 12,1906. The company deals in electrical goods, principally motors. The majority of the share capital is held by Messrs. Campos of 9 Talaat Harb Pasha Street, Alexandria.

Office and Sales Shop: 49 Avenue Fouad I, Alexandria.

Cairo Branch: 21 Cherif Pasha Street.

Capital:
£12,864 (L.E. 12,542) divided into 3,216 ordinanry shares of £4 each, fully paid.
4,500 Founders shares of no par value.
Initial share capital was £50,000 in 12,500 Ordinary £4 shares. Capital was reduced by repurchases to £38,000 in 1908, to £36,000 in 1910, to £31,840 in 1911, to £29,840 in 1917 and to £17,904 in 1923 by repayment of 2,984 shares. In 1930, there was a further reduction to £17,500 by repurchases and to £14,000 the same year by cancellation as a result of losses. Eventually, repurchases were resumed, reducing the capital to £13,344 in 1935 and to £12,864 in 1937.

SOCIÉTÉ GÉNÉRALE D'ÉLECTRICITÉ ET DE MÉCANIQUE

SOCIÉTÉ ANONYME

Autorisée par Décret Khédivial en date du 12 Mai 1906

CAPITAL SOCIAL: 50.000 Lstg

Divisé en 12.500 Actions de Quatre Livres Sterling chacune

UNE PART DE FONDATEUR AU PORTEUR

No 00,128

SOCIÉTÉ GÉNÉRALE D'ÉLECTRICITÉ & DE MÉCANIQUE · ALEXANDRIE-EGYPTE

Alexandrie, le 15 Janvier 1907

UN ADMINISTRATEUR

UN ADMINISTRATEUR·

SOCIÉTÉ GÉNÉRALE D'ÉLECTRICITÉ & DE MÉCANIQUE · ALEXANDRIE-EGYPTE

IMP. BOUR. (A. Dupat, Succr) PARIS

The making of Koubbeh Gardens

In 1904-8, Cairo witnessed an unprecedented real estate boom. It seemed like new suburbs were being created every day, the better known being Zamalek, Garden City, Heliopolis and Maadi. Smaller suburbs were also conceived in Giza, on the island of al-Roda, and within a small distance from the Khedivial palace of Koubbeh.

The latter was left to a group of well-known entrepreneurs spearheaded by Mansour Shakour Pasha. The Koubbeh Gardens Building Land Company, with Shakour as its first chairman, was created in 1907. Among its first directors were Selim Schmeil, Leon Rolin and Gaston Briere. While the latter two were Belgian businessmen with Rolin heading one of the largest contracting companies in Egypt, Shakour Pasha and Schmeil were of Syrian stock with origins in or near Mount Lebanon. Naturally, Shakour and Rolin owned Koubbeh's handsomest homes with Rolin's oriental palace standing in as a depository for Egypt's finest private collection of ancient Persian and Greek ceramics.

Capitalized at L.E. 300,000, Koubbeh Gardens Co. launched a share issue of 75,000 shares worth LE 4 pounds each. In December 1908, the capital was increased to LE 360,000 with 15,000 additional shares traded on the Cairo Exchange.

The original 96 feddans (acres) which formed the nucleus of Koubbeh Gardens were situated between the precinct of Demerdash and Koubbeh Bridge, in other words west of the older district Abbasia. By 1910, Koubbeh Gardens was home to 14 villas and one shop, 23 more feddans were added to the original tract that year. The mood was upbeat.

Unfortunately for Shakour and his colleagues, poor investments in a mortgage company in Belgium coupled with unfavorable exchange rates would take their toll. Declining sales during WWI resulted in an overall dismal performance between 1916 and 1923. As if that were not enough, the insolvency of several villa-owners obliged the company to foreclose on some properties it had recently sold in installments.

The price of the square metre, which had peaked at L.E. 0.84 in 1919, tumbled to L.E. 0.70 in 1922. Likewise, company shares were now valued at L.E 2.40. In other words, they had lost half their market value. Koubbeh Gardens Co. was in dire straits. The company went into receivership in 1926-7.

Shakour Pasha, a London University graduate (1885) with a degree in engineering, first found employment with the Egyptian State Railway (ESR), he was promoted to the post of Principal Inspector in 1902 before assuming the position of ESR's Chief of the Electrical and Telegraphic Department. He resigned in 1905 and joined the private sector with plans to develop several new Cairo suburbs. Koubbeh Gardens was one of them. As a reward for both his excellent government service record as well as his far-sighted vision, Shakour Bey received the title of Pasha in 1906.

Société d' Ameublement Krieger

Founded in 1923 as branch of Krieger Paris to manufacture and sell furniture.

Head Office: 41 Kasr el-Nil Street, Cairo.

Capital:
L.E. 55,000 divided into 5500 shares of L.E. 10 each, expiring 5 January 1951. In 1931, a reduction of capital to L.E. 27,500 took place.

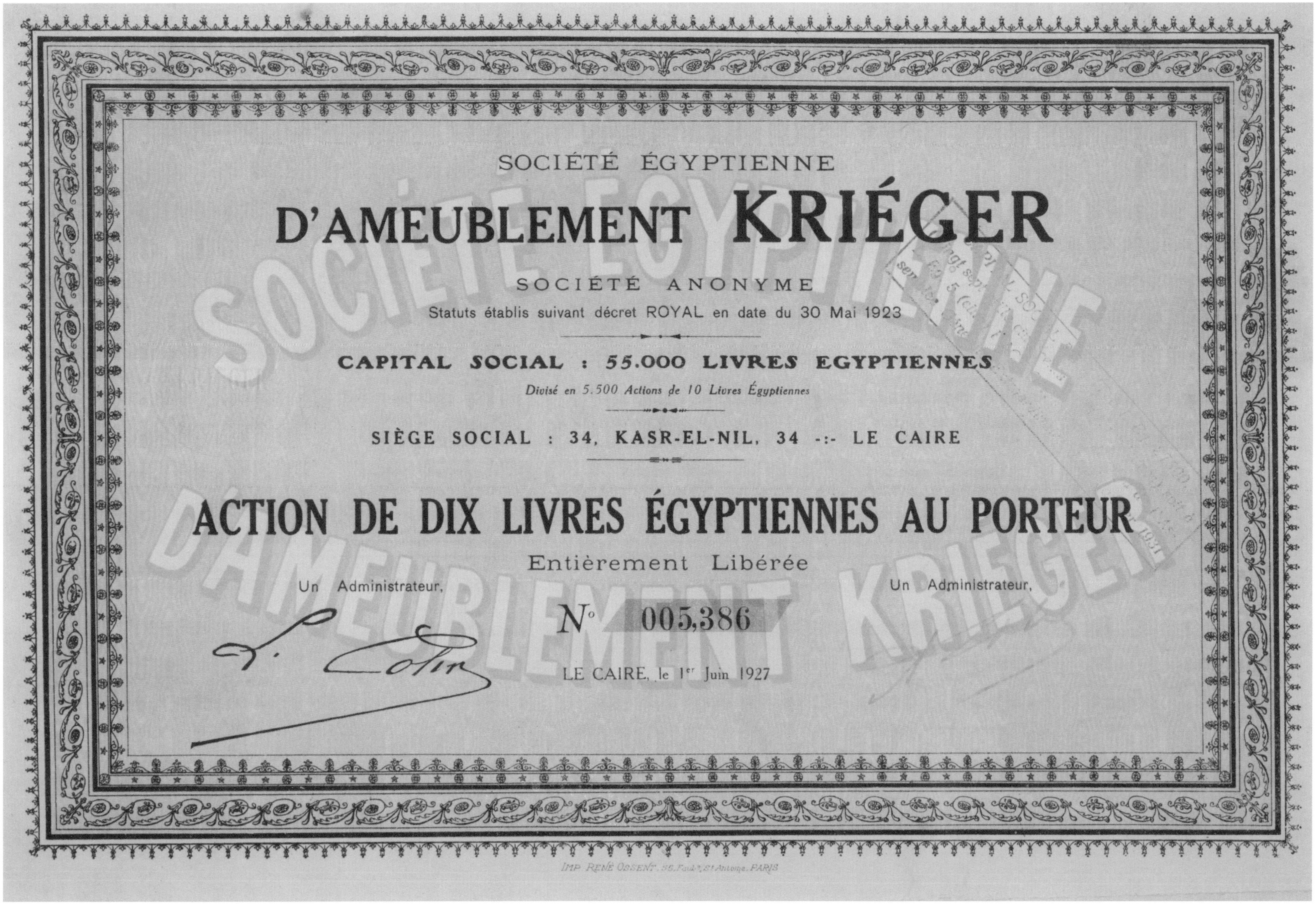

SOCIÉTÉ ÉGYPTIENNE

D'AMEUBLEMENT KRIÉGER

SOCIÉTÉ ANONYME

Statuts établis suivant décret ROYAL en date du 30 Mai 1923

CAPITAL SOCIAL : 55.000 LIVRES EGYPTIENNES

Divisé en 5.500 Actions de 10 Livres Égyptiennes

SIÈGE SOCIAL : 34, KASR-EL-NIL, 34 -:- LE CAIRE

ACTION DE DIX LIVRES ÉGYPTIENNES AU PORTEUR

Entièrement Libérée

Un Administrateur, | Un Administrateur,

N° 005,386

LE CAIRE, le 1er Juin 1927

IMP. RENÉ OSSENT, 55, Faubg St Antoine, PARIS

For an insight into the making of Koubbeh Gardens, we refer to the notes of Shakour Pasha, dated 6 March 1912, luckily preserved by his daughter Aline:

> Koubbeh Gardens is the new quarter of Cairo bordering on the northern limit of the town. It is only three and a half miles from Opera Square and yet it as quiet and healthy as though it were situated a hundred miles from the capital.
>
> During the last twenty years, Cairo has increased in the same proportion as any other capital of a prosperous country. As the government did not control the general lines on which new quarters were developed, for reasons we need not enter into, these suburbs soon became too thickly built.
>
> The intrusion of commercial and business elements of an unfavorable nature made these recent quarters lose by degrees whatever attractions they may have possessed as residential suburbs. Thus the opening of grocer and butcher shops, furniture stores, etc. all of a rather inferior order, has effectively spoilt the various suburbs of Fagalla, Abbassieh, Obesi and Tewfikieh. The Kasr al-Dubara quarter alone remains an exception to this rule, the reason being that the land belonged to government and stringent rules were laid down for its development. For this reason, the value of land in this quarter rose to prohibitive prices. Even now, though prices have fallen considerably owing to the financial crisis, building land at Kasr al-Dubara stands from four pounds to six pounds the metre, which for a residential villa and garden is beyond the means of all but the richest.
>
> It was precisely in order to meet the need of affordable housing that Koubbeh Gardens was created.
>
> The Matarieh railway embankment has served as an effective barrier to the spread of the town in a northerly direction and land on the north side of the railway was still green fields when on the town side every square foot had been built over.
>
> The advantage of this site, which became eventually Koubbeh Gardens, were the following: The soil was dry and healthy and consisted of good arable land most suitable for gardens and tree plantations. It was far enough from the Nile and consequently free of mosquitoes, mists and noxious emanations in summer at low Nile. The property was also close to Cairo, being only three and a half miles from the centre. And lastly it lies to the north of the town, a most essential consideration in Egypt, for during eight months of the year the cool breeze, without which life would be intolerable during the hot weather, comes from the north. Every house built in Egypt faces north, if possible, and every town in Egypt, without a single exception that we know of, spreads when developing towards the north.
>
> As this building site was such a favorable one, negotiations were entered into with the government to build a sub-way (under pass) under the Matarieh railway, thus rendering the site accessible to the town. After considerable difficulty, this important work was carried out at a cost of over 22,000 pounds and is the finest sub-way in Egypt.
>
> As the land in this locality belonged to many small proprietors, there was great difficulty in purchasing it; the whole estate, which is now one longitudinal area, consisted of no less than 80 holdings.

Société Egyptienne d'Entreprises Urbaines & Rurales

Registered on April 27, 1905. The company owns building properties in Alexandria at 44 Ishak el-Nadim Street, 22 Moharrem Bey Street and 19 Rue de France, as well as building sites in different parts of Alexandria and a half share in an estate acquired from the Wakf el-Guizami at Giza, Cairo. This estate of 22½ feddans was purchased in 1946 at the price of L.E. 2,660 per feddan.

Head Office: 44 Ishak al-Nadim Street Street, Alexandria.

Capital:
£200,000 divided into 50,000 Ordinary shares of £4 each, fully paid.
3,000 Founders shares of no par value.

SOCIÉTÉ D'ENTREPRISES URBAINES & RURALES
ALEXANDRIE EGYPTE

TWO SHILLINGS

SOCIÉTÉ EGYPTIENNE D'ENTREPRISES URBAINES & RURALES

SOCIÉTÉ ANONYME AUTORISÉE PAR DÉCRET KHÉDIVIAL EN DATE DU 27 AVRIL 1905

Publié au *Journal Officiel*, N° 53, du 8 Mai 1905 et constituée le 9 Mai 1905.

LE CAPITAL SOCIAL A ÉTÉ PORTÉ A L. Stg. 400.000 PAR LA CRÉATION DE 25.000 ACTIONS NOUVELLES

CAPITAL SOCIAL 300.000 L. stg.

DIVISÉ EN 75.000 ACTIONS DE L.STG. QUATRE CHACUNE

Les Statuts de la Société ont été déposés le 9 Mai 1905, sub N° 467, au Tribunal du Commerce Mixte d'Alexandrie et publiés le 10 Mai 1905 au journal d'annonces légales, à Alexandrie, *La Réforme*.

SIÈGE SOCIAL À ALEXANDRIE

TITRE AU PORTEUR

10 ACTIONS — de Dix Actions de Livres Stg Quatre chacune — 40 LSTG.

ENTIÈREMENT LIBÉRÉES

N° 19311 À N° 19320

UN ADMINISTRATEUR — UN ADMINISTRATEUR

Titre non négociable fait partie des actions rachetées et annulées le … juin 1910

Alexandrie le 1er Juin 1905

ANNULÉ

TIP. LITH. I. DELLA ROCCA ALEX.

SOCIÉTÉ ÉGYPTIENNE D'ENTREPRISES URBAINES & RURALES — DIX ACTIONS — N° 19311 A N° 19320 — 50 Coupon payable au porteur 50 — ANNULÉ

SOCIÉTÉ ÉGYPTIENNE D'ENTREPRISES URBAINES & RURALES — DIX ACTIONS — N° 19311 A N° 19320 — 49 Coupon payable au porteur 49 — ANNULÉ

SOCIÉTÉ ÉGYPTIENNE D'ENTREPRISES URBAINES & RURALES — DIX ACTIONS — N° 19311 A N° 19320 — 48 Coupon payable au porteur 48 — ANNULÉ

SOCIÉTÉ ÉGYPTIENNE D'ENTREPRISES URBAINES & RURALES — DIX ACTIONS — N° 19311 A N° 19320 — 47 Coupon payable au porteur 47 — ANNULÉ

SOCIÉTÉ ÉGYPTIENNE D'ENTREPRISES URBAINES & RURALES — DIX ACTIONS — N° 19311 A N° 19320 — 46 Coupon payable au porteur 46 — ANNULÉ

SOCIÉTÉ ÉGYPTIENNE D'ENTREPRISES URBAINES & RURALES — DIX ACTIONS — N° 19311 A N° 19320 — 45 Coupon payable au porteur 45 — ANNULÉ

SOCIÉTÉ ÉGYPTIENNE D'ENTREPRISES URBAINES & RURALES — DIX ACTIONS — N° 19311 A N° 19320 — 44 Coupon payable au porteur 44 — ANNULÉ

SOCIÉTÉ ÉGYPTIENNE D'ENTREPRISES URBAINES & RURALES — DIX ACTIONS — N° 19311 A N° 19320 — 43 Coupon payable au porteur 43 — ANNULÉ

SOCIÉTÉ ÉGYPTIENNE D'ENTREPRISES URBAINES & RURALES — DIX ACTIONS — N° 19311 A N° 19320 — 42 Coupon payable au porteur 42 — ANNULÉ

SOCIÉTÉ ÉGYPTIENNE D'ENTREPRISES URBAINES & RURALES — DIX ACTIONS — N° 19311 A N° 19320 — 41 Coupon payable au porteur 41 — ANNULÉ

SOCIÉTÉ ÉGYPTIENNE D'ENTREPRISES URBAINES & RURALES

By arrangement with the government, the main collector of the new Cairo drainage scheme passes under the whole length of the beautiful Koubbeh Gardens Avenue rendering the quarter the healthiest in Egypt. This collector took two years to build and has just been completed.

The main avenue, which is 3.5 kilometres long, is no less than 20 metres broad. It is bordered on each side by trees, of which about 1800 have been planted in Koubbeh Gardens. By special permission of His Highness the Khedive, the Avenue has been named Sharia El Khedewi (Avenue of the Khedive), and this is the road H.H. uses when going to Cairo from his palace at Koubbeh.

Arrangements have been made with the Gas, Electric Light and Water Companies of Cairo, and their mains are now laid. The prices charged for water —a very necessary item in Egypt — is considerably less than in town.

It should also be mentioned that this quarter is connected with the centre of Cairo by means of the Heliopolis Oases Railway and the Matarieh Railway. The station of the former is at Demerdash close to the sub-way, and a convenient half-hour service affords a ready means for getting into Cairo. The Matarieh Railway has three stations along the line, each of which is within five minutes walk from the Koubbeh Gardens. Besides this, the Koubbeh Gardens Company has obtained authorisation to run a motor-bus service connecting the Estate directly with Opera Square.

The success of Heliopolis is a sure guarantee of what can be done at Koubbeh Garden, which enjoys so many more advantages, chiefly those of being closer to town and possessing a soil that will grow vegetation of every kind at a very small expense. All that is required is funds for building. The 25 or 30 villas already built on the estate are all occupied, and there are many applications for more.

The last annual report of the Board of Directors shows the financial situation of the Company. Since its issue, completing the roads and new buildings has absorbed nearly all available funds.

The conditions for purchase, copy of which is annexed, impose restrictions, the object being to keep the locality an advantageous one from a residential point of view.

With considerable hindsight, Shakour Pasha was overly enthusiastic about the prospects of his suburban brainchild. Optimism that often surpassed his company's financial statements — at times the figures in his 1912 notes did not tally with the related Annual Reports. Sadly, time would prove him wrong, for among the many suburbs that were created at the turn of 20th century, Koubbeh Gardens was the first to suffer irreversible decline and for the very same reasons he evoked in the third paragraph of his revealing notes.

The Delta Trading Company

Formerly S. G. Rabbath

The Delta Trading Company was registered on June 8, 1920, dealing in agricultural and industrial machinery, building materials and iron and steel products, with workshops in Cairo and Alexandria.

Head Office: 18 Emad-el-Din Street, Cairo
Branch: 78 Avenue Fouad I (for building materials)

Capital:
L.E. 750,000 divided into 187,500 Ordinary shares of L.E. 4 each, fully paid.

10 ACTIONS

L.E. 40

THE DELTA TRADING COMPANY

SOCIÉTÉ ANONYME ÉGYPTIENNE

Autorisée par Décret du 8 Juin 1920, promulguée au Journal Officiel du 15 Juillet 1920.

SIÈGE SOCIAL : ALEXANDRIE (EGYPTE)

CAPITAL SOCIAL : 500.000 LIVRES ÉGYPTIENNES

REPRÉSENTÉ PAR 125.000 ACTIONS DE 4 LIVRES ÉGYPTIENNES CHACUNE.

THE DELTA TRADING CY. S.A.E.
LE CAIRE
CAPITAL AUGMENTÉ DE L.E. 500.000.- à L.E. 750.000
Droit exercé.

TITRE DE DIX ACTIONS AU PORTEUR

DE 4 LIVRES ÉGYPTIENNES CHACUNE

Un Administrateur, Nos 69031 à 69040 Un Administrateur,

ENTIÈREMENT LIBÉRÉES

Alexandrie, le 29 Juin 1944.

LITH Fres VENTURA ALEXANDRIE

The Delta Trading Company
Société Anonyme Egyptienne
TITRE DE DIX ACTIONS
DE 4 LIVRES EGYPTIENNES
Nos 69031 à 69040
Après paiement du coupon No. 59, contre la remise du présent talon, il sera remis une nouvelle feuille de coupons. La présentation du titre pourra être exigée.

The Delta Trading Company
Société Anonyme Egyptienne
TITRE DE DIX ACTIONS
DE 4 LIVRES EGYPTIENNES
Nos 69031 à 69040
COUPON DE DIVIDENDE
59 58 57 56 55 54 53 52 51

Finneyland

In Dokki, one often hears the nearby *midan* (traffic roundabout) referred to as Midan Finney. Not only was Midan Sad al-Aali originally Midan Finney, but Sad al-Aali Street which intersects the entire neighborhood of western Dokki was for more than three decades known as rue Finney. The Alexandria-born Mr. Finney, whenever in Cairo, lived in a large villa overlooking "his" midan.

Finney's house is still there today but in the corrupted guise of a hospital. Acquired by Ahmed Hassan Pasha, Villa Finney was sold to the Chabrawichi family who turned it into a hospital thus making it the second such institution fronting the midan. Anouss Hospital, specializing in ENT, had made its debut a few years earlier. (Anouss Hospital was pulled down in 1997). Soon would appear not far from Midan Finney, the hospitals of Doctors Ali Ibrahim and Abdallah Kateb. For some time during the 1950s, this part of Cairo was characterized as an upmarket medical center for the rich and famous.

The Finneys (Oswald and his wife Josa) were among the leading British families of Alexandria. A major figure in the cotton trade, Oswald J. Finney was well known not only for some of the world's finest tapestries that festooned the walls of his five-floor hotel particulier at No. 3 Rolo Street, but also for being the town's top publisher and reportedly one of its wealthiest men. Likewise, he sat on the board of several giant cotton trading companies in both Alexandria and Lancashire (UK). More importantly Finney, was the sometime president of the Alexandria Commercial Company, the Alexandria Insurance Company, the Filature Nationale d'Égypte and the Minet al-Bassal Stock Exchange.

In Cairo, Oswald Finney was also president of the Société Anonyme Immobiliere des Terrains de Giza & Rodah, the real estate development company that in the 1920s and 1930s surveyed and laid out the master plan for what became the suburban garden districts of Rodah Island, the southern part of Agouza and all of Dokki.

This real estate development company was created by the Rodochanachi-Zervudachi scions back in 1908 when most of the land west of the Nile in the Cairo area was either state property or in the hands of the members of the Khedivial family. These were the real-estate boom years that saw the creation of Garden City, Heliopolis, Maadi and Zamalek. As a result of mismanagement of funds and a notorious financial scandal, the Giza & Rodah Co. was forced into bankruptcy and by 1910 was put into receivership. Ultimately acquired by Oswald Finney and his associates, the new owners decided to postpone development for almost a decade save for limited construction, mostly along the Nile.

The bulk of the soon-to-become fashionable suburb of Dokki's development commenced in the mid 1930s accompanied by an aggressive marketing campaign spearheaded by Tréhaki, Pilavachi & Co. acting as official real estate agents. Advertisements announced favorable installment payments, cheap financing and excellent mortgage terms. Since Finney owned the Société Orientale de Publicité, many such promos appeared in his

The Alexandria Insurance Company

Registered on May 29, 1928 and founded by Amin Yehia Pasha, transacting all kinds of insurance and reinsurance, except life insurance.

Head Office: 12, Boulevard Zaghloul, Alexandria.

Capital:
Subscribed L.E. 360,000 divided into 3,600 Ordinanry shares of L.E. 10 each. Paid-up L.E. 90,000 (or L.E. 25 per L.E. 100 share).

20 ACTIONS

٢٠ سهما

PAR ORDRE بأمر

شركة اسكندرية للتأمين

شركة مساهمة مصرية

مؤسسها الأمين يحيى باشا

مرخص بها بمرسوم ملكي في ٢٩ مايو سنة ١٩٢٨

The Alexandria Insurance Company

Société Anonyme Egyptienne — Fondée par Emin Yehia Pacha

Autorisée par Décret Royal du 29 Mai 1928

Siège Social : ALEXANDRIE

CAPITAL SOCIAL : L.E. 180.000

DIVISÉ EN 36,000 ACTIONS NOMINATIVES
DE L.EG. 5 CHACUNE ENTIÈREMENT LIBÉRÉES

TITRE NOMINATIF DE
VINGT ACTIONS

المركز الرئيسي : الاسكندرية

رأس المال : ١٨٠،٠٠٠ جنيه مصري

مقسم إلى ٣٦٠٠٠ سهم اسمي

قيمة كل منها ٥ جنيهات مصرية مدفوعة بالكامل

سند اسمي
بعشرين سهما

Inscrit au nom de M خاصة جلالة الملك

مقيد باسم حضرة

عضو مجلس الادارة
UN ADMINISTRATEUR

N° 03101 à N° 03120

عضو مجلس الادارة
UN ADMINISTRATEUR

Alexandrie Janvier 1950 الاسكندرية في يناير سنة ١٩٥٠

100 L. EG.

١٠٠ جنيه مصري

SOCIÉTÉ DE PUBLICATIONS EGYPTIENNES

publications including Le Progrés Egyptien, the Egyptian Gazette and La Bourse Egyptienne. Following his death in September 1942, his son looked after the family business along with the various company directorships.

This particular piece of suburban development was labeled the English Bridge layout, a reference to the nearby *Kobri al-Ingiliz*. It had pre-determined boundaries: Avenue Khedive Ismail (now Tahrir Street) to the south; the curvy Abdel Rehim Sabry to the west; Avenue Wezaret al-Zira'a (Nawal) to the north; and Avenue Bahr al Aama a.k.a. Farouk al-Awwal Avenue (now Agouza Nile Corniche) to the east. Within these parametres is Finneyland, an oasis of grand mansions and charming villas with gardens.

First there were the palatial Nile-front homes of Chamseldine Abdel Ghafaar Pasha (purchased later by cabaret queen Madame Badia Masabni), Boulos Hanna Pasha (Cairo Far East Bank), Galal Ezzat Bey (Finnish Embassy) and Senator Abdel Aziz Radwan.

Nearby but slightly removed from the Nile Corniche, we find the remakrable house of Salem Hindawi (also spelt Hindaoui) Pasha whose first wife Khayreya Hanem was lady in waiting to Queen Nazli (the widowed Hindawi would later marry Hanifa Shafik).

Dr. Hindawi's house is a vivid example of Islamic revival possibly inspired by the neo-Mamluk style Ministry of Awqaf headquarters on Gamea Sharkass Street where Hindawi occupied the post of medical director. Among Hindawi's more renowned patients circa 1926 features Prince (later King) Seoud Ibn Abdel Aziz of Saudi Arabia who at a very early age suffered from eye disease which later make his distinctive dark glasses world famous.

Further inland, fronting or close to Midan Finney, we find the villas leased to or belonging to the Diwanis, Elouis, Hamamas, Hilmis and Sirrys next to the Argys, Bialobos, Bondis, Carmonas, Cicurels, Cohencas, Gattegnos, Hettenas, Molhos and Sullams. All belonged to the haute bourgeoisie and top-drawer merchant class. While the first group is composed of mainly white-collar Egyptian civil servants and technocrats, the second group represents a sample of the wealthier Sefardi families specialized in the retail, electric and small firearms trade.

Down rue Finney past the midan, we find the house where Camelia (Liliane Cohen) lived neatly sandwiched between Villa Debbas overlooking the midan and the three-floor Ciskovich building later acquired by Hag Agatti, the renowned silversmith. Camelia was King Farouk's favorite starlet before she died tragically in the TWA plane crash near Wadi Natrun.

Fronting rue Finney were the homes of noted Greeks and Italians including Dr. Socrates Thomaides (Villa Roula) and Madame Grazia who gave dancing classes attended by her neighbors Poppy Papastephanou, Roula Thomaides and Alice Bondi along with other neighborhood ladies. Behind Villa Roula on Abdel Rehim Sabry Street was the house of Nicola Kerestezoglu whose emporium at No. 11 Soliman Pasha sold the finest oriental carpets.

Foremost among the prominent Egyptians residing in Finneyland when the entire area was still known as Bulak al-Dakrour was King Farouk's grandfather Abdel Rehim Sabry Pasha. His vast property — Nawal — consisting of

The National Salt & Mining Co.

Registered on April 18th, 1949. The company was granted the sole right to work Governemnt salt mines at Mex, Menessi and Baltim.

Head Office: 41 Nebi Daniel Street, Alexandria.

Capital:
L.E. 100,000 divided into 25,000 Ordinary shares of L.E. 4 each fully paid.

N·S&M·Co

40 £

٤٠ جنيه مصري

شركة الملح والتعدين الأهلية

شركة مساهمة مصرية

THE NATIONAL SALT & MINING Co.

SOCIÉTÉ ANONYME EGYPTIENNE

Autorisée par Décret Royal du 18 Avril 1949

تأسست بمرسوم ملكي بتاريخ ١٨ ابريل سنة ١٩٤٩

Siège Social:
ALEXANDRIE (Egypte)

مركزها الأسكندرية

CAPITAL AUTORISÉ L.E. 100.000
DIVISÉ EN 25.000 ACTIONS DE L.E. 4 CHACUNE

رأس المال المصرح به ١٠٠٠٠٠ جنيه مصري
مقسم الى ٢٥٠٠٠ سهم قيمة السهم الواحد اربعة جنيهات مصرية

TITRE AU PORTEUR DE
DIX ACTIONS
ENTIÈREMENT LIBÉRÉES

سند
بعشرة اسهم لحامله
مدفوعة بأكملها

عضو مجلس الادارة
UN ADMINISTRATEUR

No. 11231 À No. 11240

رئيس مجلس الادارة
LE PRÉSIDENT

Alexandrie le 18 Avril 1949.

الاسكندرية في ١٨ ابريل ١٩٤٩

10 ACTIONS

اسهم

a mansion and an unique park extended along a large part of the street named after him. Stephan Papastephanou remembers how, as a young boy, he watched from the family balcony as the red and black Rolls Royce passed back and forth from the Sabry mansion which was separated from his own house by the beautiful Gategno residence. "Whenever Queen Nazli was in residence many dignitaries visited her including the Shah of Iran when he was married to her daughter Princess Fawzia. A policeman was usually stationed at the corner of Finney and Abdel Rehim Sabry streets."

The other three other notables who lent their names to Finneyland streets were ophtalmologist Salem Hindawi, Boulos Hanna Pasha and Ismail Bey Aboul Fetouh. The Ministry of Culture is the present owner of the latter's villa. Meanwhile Abul Ezz Pasha acquired the nearby Villa Debbas. Other urban survivors include the handsome villa of Zakaria Mahraan Pasha purchased by Osman Abdel Ghafaar before it became home to Kuwait's ambassadors starting with Hamad al-Rujaib.

Many villas didn't make it and were replaced by unsavory high-rises during the free-for-all 1970s and '80s. One of the first victims was No. 128 Farouk al-Awwal Avenue, the mansion designed by Italian architect Romollo Gilardini in the 1920s and which, during WWII, became a convalescence home for British soldiers courtesy of its munificent owner, Abdel Aziz Radwan Pasha. In return, the pasha's male progeny were graciously welcomed in some of Britain's top schools.

Thankfully, on Boulos Hanna Street West still stands a smoldering cluster of Finneyland's finest homes. Grandest among them is that other mansion designed by Gilardini in 1931, this time for Ali Sadek Bey. This wonderful piece of faux-renaissance with tennis court, fish grotto and the 30 orderlies needed to run it was subsequently purchased by mega-landowner Sayed Badrawi Pasha before becoming many years later the Wafd Party's dilapidated headquarters.

Next to Sadek Bey's Italian folly stands the lesser palazzo of Upper Egypt millionaire Mohammed Sultan. With his Jewish wife Laure Menashe, the debonair pasha entertained le-tout-post-WWII-Caire until the 1952 coup put an end to it all. Today it is home to the South Korean Embassy.

Also on Boulos Hanna West is the quaint home of exiled Moroccan chieftain Abdel Salaam Khatabi standing opposite the elegant immeuble de rapport (Villa Akmar No. 5) designed by Naoum Chebib of Cairo Tower fame for veteran Egyptologist Charles Kuentz (1895-1978). Nearby is the villa of Madame Labib Pasha Attia, until 2008 the Algerian Embassy residence.

The last Finney to reside in Finneyland was Oswald's son Harold Edward. He left Egypt in 1956. All that remains of the Finney legacy in Dokki today is a small hospital by the same name, Finney Hospital at No. 26 Abdel Rehim Sabry Pasha Street.

Dr. Salem Hindawi Pasha Street changed to Dr. Abdallah Kateb Street. Ismail Aboul Fetouh Street changed to

Société Egyptienne de Tissage et Tricotage

Registered on December 13, 1934. The company owned an artificial silk and cotton weaving factory at Shubra, Cairo, equipped with 137 looms and 14 knitting machines. The Filature Nationale d'Egypte held 5,000 shares in this company.

Office: 1 Borsa el-Gedida Street, Cairo.

Capital:
L.E. 200,000 divided into 50,000 Ordinary shares of L.E. 4 each, fully paid.

9963

Société Egyptienne de Tissage et Tricotage

N° du Titre 0086

Société Egyptienne de Tissage et Tricotage

Société Anonyme Egyptienne

Autorisée par Décret Royal en date du 13 Décembre 1934

AU CAPITAL DE L.E. 24.000

porté à L.E. 30.000

par décision de l'Assemblée Générale Extraordinaire du 14 Mars 1935

DIVISÉ EN 7500 ACTIONS DE L.E. 4 CHACUNE

1 ACTION

L.Eg. 4

UNE ACTION AU PORTEUR

DE LIVRES EGYPTIENNES QUATRE

N° 0086

Le Caire, le 11 Avril 1935

UN ADMINISTRATEUR

UN ADMINISTRATEUR

Capital porté à Quarante Mille Livres Egyptiennes par décision de l'Assemblée Générale Extraordinaire du 26 Mars 1936. Droit de préférence 30.3. 6.4.1936.

Capital porté à L.E. 75.000 suivant décision de l'Assemblée Générale Extraordinaire du 24 Avril 1942 et du Conseil d'Administration du 29 Octobre 1942 - Droit de préférence - 1er Novembre 1942 - 15 Décembre 1942.

Capital porté à Cent Vingt Cinq Mille Livres Egyptiennes par décision de l'Assemblée Générale Extraordinaire du 20 Mars 1944 - Droit de préférence 20 Mars 1944.

Capital porté à Deux Cent Mille Livres Egyptiennes par décision de l'Assemblée Générale Extraordinaire du 15 Janvier 1945. Droit de préférence du 1er Février au 16 Février 1945.

TYPO LITHO. FLLI. VENTURA, ALEX.

SOCIÉTÉ ÉGYPTIENNE DE TISSAGE ET TRICOTAGE SOCIÉTÉ ANONYME UNE ACTION N° 0086 COUPON PAYABLE AU PORTEUR 50	SOCIÉTÉ ÉGYPTIENNE DE TISSAGE ET TRICOTAGE SOCIÉTÉ ANONYME UNE ACTION N° 0086 COUPON PAYABLE AU PORTEUR 49	SOCIÉTÉ ÉGYPTIENNE DE TISSAGE ET TRICOTAGE SOCIÉTÉ ANONYME UNE ACTION N° 0086 COUPON PAYABLE AU PORTEUR 48	SOCIÉTÉ ÉGYPTIENNE DE TISSAGE ET TRICOTAGE SOCIÉTÉ ANONYME UNE ACTION N° 0086 COUPON PAYABLE AU PORTEUR 47	SOCIÉTÉ ÉGYPTIENNE DE TISSAGE ET TRICOTAGE SOCIÉTÉ ANONYME UNE ACTION N° 0086 COUPON PAYABLE AU PORTEUR 46

Kuwait Street. The mansion of Abdel Rehim Sabry Pasha was confiscated by the state and transformed into the Nasser Higher Military Academy. Villa Kerestezoglu No. 30 Abdel Rehim Sabry Pasha Street is now headquarter of SEPEI Co. Gategno House No. 36 Abdel Rehim Sabry Pasha Street is now the residence of the Syrian ambassador. Villa No. 114 Giza Corniche was completely restored in 2004 by its new owner businessman Aboul Enein. The twin George Zananiri (a.k.a. Messawer) Buildings No. 124 & 126 Giza Corniche are still extant. Villa Guy Cicurel on Boulos Hanna Street West is now the residence of the Dutch ambassador.

Regarding the entomology of "Agouza" and mosque by the same name, I hold over to Mahmoud Adel Sabit who has meticulously chronicled his family's history:

> The mosque was built with funds provided by Nazli al-Fransawi (wife of statesman Cherif Pasha). In view of its size, the Nazli *wakfiya* (endownment/trust) was divided into two parts. Items that were supposed to benefit from the wakfiya include those structures that Nazli had constructed:
>
> (i) mausoleum of Cherif Pasha;
>
> (ii) mausoleum of her father Soliman Pasha;
>
> (iii) mosque at Agouza which incorporates a *madrassa* (school) and library
>
> (iv) mosque in Talla, Minoufia.
>
> Because of her daily visits to her Giza opus during its construction in 1910, the workmen dubbed it *al-Agouza* (old lady) Mosque in view of Nazli's advanced age. With the passage of time and the development of an urban landscape, the quarter took the name of the mosque.
>
> The land where the mosque is located was once part of the estate of Mohamed Cherif al-Soghayar (junior). Upon the death of Mohammed, the only son of Cherif Pasha, his estate was divided between his mother, his two sisters, and a couple of other relatives. His sister Tewfika was married to Abdel Rehim Sabry Pasha who built the palace Nawal on her portion of the land. The name is attributed to Tewfika's departed daughter.
>
> Whereas the mosque is known today as Masjid al-Agouza, it was originally called Masjid Nazli Cherif. A smaller mosque further north attached to the village of al-Agouza al Westania (westania=middle) was called al-Agouza Mosque preceding the present one by several decades.
>
> The village of al-Agouza al-Ganoubia (South) was located where the 6th of October Bridge reaches Giza. Both these villages did not exist when the Nile's western bank was located further west next to the Agricultural Museum.

Usines Réunies d'Egrenage & d'Huileries

Registered on March 24, 1923. The company owned a cotton-seed oil refinery and ginning factory at Mit Ghamr, Lower Egypt. With a commercial branch for the general purchase and sale of cotton and cotton-seed, it also made advances on cotton.

Head Office: 164, Promenade Reine Nazli, Alexandria.

Capital:
L.E. 150,000 divided into 37,500 Ordinary shares of L.E.4 each, fully paid. In June 1945, capital was increased from L.E. 100,0000 to L.E. 150,000.

1 ACTION

L.E. 4

USINES RÉUNIES D'EGRENAGE & D'HUILERIES

...écision de l'Assem...
...du 9 Décembre 19...
...a été réduit d...
...000.- par l'annulation et le rembou...
...de 12500 actions de L.Eg. 4.- chaque

SOCIÉTÉ ANONYME EGYPTIENNE

AUTORISÉE PAR DÉCRET ROYAL EN DATE DU 24 MARS 1923

CONSTITUÉE AU CAPITAL DE L. EG. 60.000

CAPITAL SOCIAL ACTUEL LIVRES EGYPTIENNES 100.000

DIVISÉ EN 25.000 ACTIONS DE L. Eg. 4 CHACUNE

ENTIÈREMENT LIBÉRÉES

SUIVANT DÉLIBÉRATION DE L'ASSEMBLÉE GÉNÉRALE EXTRAORDINAIRE DU 12 MAI 1923

SIÈGE SOCIAL: ALEXANDRIE

Agence MIT-GHAMR

UNE ACTION AU PORTEUR

DE L. Eg. QUATRE

UN ADMINISTRATEUR

Nº 00496

UN ADMINISTRATEUR

Alexandrie, Septembre 1923

1 ACTION

L.E. 4

TYPO-LITHO. FLLI. VENTURA. ALEX.

The Baehler Skyline

One of Charles Baehler's last creations was the downtown Baehler Buildings which overlook Soliman Pasha (now Talaat Harb) Square. Built between 1927-29, these deluxe tenements replaced the Savoy Hotel and its attachments which included the Savoy Chambers.

The Savoy had long been one of colonial Cairo's most important business and residential addresses. It was there that British-owned companies established their representative offices and it was at the smart Savoy Hotel that the British army set up its GHQ during WWI.

Barely three decades old, the Savoy complex was pulled down in 1924 by its new owner. Charles Baehler cleared the way for his own personal understanding of what an interdisciplinary urban construction should be. Nothing of that scale had yet been seen in downtown Cairo. And if the city center lost one of its leading hotels, the father of Egypt's hospitality industry superseded the Savoy with the neo-classic Metropolitan (later renamed Cosmopolitan) Hotel just around the corner, off Kasr el Nil Street. True to a lifetime dedicated to hotels, the Cosmopolitan was Baehler's last contribution to Cairo's urbana.

Baehler's downtown plaza consisted of six semi-detached buildings (blocs A through F), each with its own entrance. The buildings contained 130 deluxe apartments, some conceived as offices, the rest residential. The ground floors were partitioned into 72 shops each with a separate basement. The style was fin-de-siecle Parisian.

The Baehler Arcade (or Passage, as it soon came to be called) could have been a miniature version of rue de Rivoli in Paris. Crawling with premium boutiques, the arcade sheltered the best haberdasheries, the finest lingerie, the trendiest men's wear and the artiest painting galleries in town. As for the showrooms fronting Soliman Pasha or Kasr El Nil Streets, these were game to the highest bidder.

Baehler knew a thing or two about proportion, harmony and streetscape. His commercial lease contracts spelt out in the clearest of terms the do's and don'ts regarding storefront merchandising, promotional lighting and window displays. There was no thought yet that someone would dare append a medical signpost to his balcony grill or pockmark his façade with leaking air-conditioners.

Preceding Baehler Buildings and Passage are two of the handsomest structures on Zamalek's 26th of July Street. Everyone in Zamalek has either had a pizza at Maison Thomas or purchased a cold Stella from the al-Ahram Beverages depot. Welcome to Baehler Mansions built early this century on land carved out from the former Khedivial palace gardens.

Realizing Cairo was expanding westwards towards the Nile, Baehler, owner of the Gezira Palace Hotel (today Marriott Hotel), took up his option to buy more of the island's agricultural land, to form an urban development company. The new district of Zamalek was born.

The Shepheard's and Egyptian Hotels Company

Registered in England on January 12, 1897 as hotel proprietors. The company owned the following hotels in Cairo:
1. Semiramis Hotel, freehold land and building
2. Shepheard's Hotel, built on leasehold land. The land measuring 20,700 sq. metres, is the property of the Wakf Halim from whom it was leased in 1897 for a period of 75 years up to 1972.
In addition, the company also leased three hotels from the Grands Hotels d'Egypte (ex. Nungovich), until April 30, 1950 for which it paid a total annual rental of L.E. 35,150. The hotels are: the Continental-Savoy Hotel, excluding shop premises; Mena House Hotel, Pyramids, with annex; and Grand Hotel Helwan.

The Egyptian Hotels Limited held 19,500 £1 Ordinary Shares of Palestine Hotels Limited, proprietors of the King David Hotel, Jerusalem.

Cairo Office: Shepheard's Hotel, Ibrahim Pasha St.

Capital:
Issued and Paid-up £615,000 comprising:
–£115,000 divided into 11,500 5% Ordinary Shares of £1 each.
–£500,000 divided into 500,000 Ordinary Shares of £1 each.

TITRE N° 021137 SÉRIE D

سند رقم ٠٢١١٣٧ مجموعة د

شركة شبرد والفنادق المصرية

شركة مساهمة مصرية – سجل تجارى القاهرة رقم ١٨٢

أسست سنة ١٨٩٥ وحولت إلى شركة مساهمة مصرية بموجب قرار السيد رئيس الجمهورية العربية المتحدة المؤرخ ٣٠ يوليو سنة ١٩٥٨
والمنشور بالوقائع المصرية فى العدد ٦٣ بتاريخ ١٤ أغسطس سنة ١٩٥٨ وذلك طبقا للقانون رقم ٣١٥ لسنة ١٩٥٥

THE SHEPHEARD'S & EGYPTIAN HOTELS COMPANY

SOCIÉTÉ ANONYME ÉGYPTIENNE – R.C. 182 LE CAIRE

CONSTITUÉE EN 1895 ET TRANSFORMÉE EN VERTU DE LA LOI N° 315 DE 1955 EN SOCIÉTÉ ANONYME ÉGYPTIENNE, SUIVANT DÉCISION DU PRÉSIDENT DE LA RÉPUBLIQUE ARABE UNIE DU 30 JUILLET 1958, PUBLIÉE AU JOURNAL OFFICIEL N° 63 DU 14 AOUT 1958.

CAPITAL SOCIAL L.E. 1.015.000

DIVISÉ EN 115.000 ACTIONS PRIVILÉGIÉES
ET 900.000 ACTIONS ORDINAIRES
DE L.EG. UNE CHACUNE
ENTIÈREMENT LIBÉRÉES

رأس المال ١,٠١٥,٠٠٠ جنيه مصرى

مقسم على ١١٥٠٠٠ سهم ممتاز
و ٩٠٠٠٠٠ سهم عادى
قيمة كل منها جنيه مصرى واحد
مدفوعة بالكامل

TITRE AU PORTEUR DE
VINGT-CINQ ACTIONS ORDINAIRES

سند لحامله
بخمسة وعشرين سهما عاديا

No. 665401 à No. 665425

رقم ٦٦٥٤٠١ إلى رقم ٦٦٥٤٢٥

عضو مجلس الادارة
UN ADMINISTRATEUR

J. Renou

القاهرة فى أول مايو سنة ١٩٥٩

Le Caire, le 1er Mai 1959.

عضو مجلس الادارة
UN ADMINISTRATEUR

بنك القاهرة (١٩ عدلى) القاهرة

25 ACTIONS ORD. — ٢٥ سهما — 25 L.Eg — ٢٥ جنيه مصرى

SOC. PUBLICATIONS EGYPT. ALEX.

The Swiss hotelier turned to Alex Skynder of Skynder & Skynder when he decided to build in Zamalek two grand buildings separated by a circular landing or outer court. Here too we find the splendiferous elevator cages, the lofty vaults, the ornate brickwork and the decorative details, and the endless foyers conceived in the days when capitalists weren't preoccupied with returns per square metre.

Again, Baehler would be aghast at the vulgar additions forced upon Zamalek's two grand ladies. Time has been unkind to Cairo's belle époque architecture but Monsieur Baehler may find some comfort in learning that Cairo's most photographed interior is domiciled at Baehler Mansions, home to Egypt's leading decorator Ihab Shafik.

Zamalek's Ghezireh House a.k.a. Emaret al-Yemeni, thus re-named after a latter-day owner, is also a Baehler creation. Designed in 1908-9 by Ernest Jaspar of Heliopolis fame, this building can claim to be the island's first immeuble de rapport–apartment house.

At the age of twenty-one, Swiss-born Charles Baehler arrived in Cairo on 21 October 1889. By 1904, he had acquired controlling interest in the Egyptian Hotels Limited founded in 1897, and by 1906 had formed the Upper Egypt Hotels with five hotels in Luxor and Aswan, including the Winter Palace (which he built) and the Cataract.

In 1907, he created the Electric Light and Power Supply Company which fed 2,500 horsepower worth of electricity to the Shepheards Hotel and the outlying district. In 1908, he purchased additional land on Gezira (ex-Boulac) Island and created the new urban district of Zamalek.

In 1910, he acquired controlling shares in Semiramis Hotel which he immediately enlarged. In 1925, Egyptian Hotels agreed to manage the properties of Grand Hotels Company (ex-Nungovitch Group) for 25 years. With the Continental, Mena House, Helwan and San Stefano joining the fold, Baehler was in control of most of Egypt's leading hotels with an aggregate of 4,000 beds. In 1929, he constructed the King David Hotel in Jerusalem.

Between 1927-29, he constructed Baehler Mansions in Zamalek (now owned, one each, by the Chishini family and former minister Adel Abdel-Baki) and the Baehler Buildings in downtown Cairo (now the property of Insurance companies). In 1928-9, he opened the Metropolitan (later Cosmopolitan) Hotel off Cairo's Kasr el Nil Street; and launched a small hotel in Fayoum.

An avid art collector and sportsman, Baehler was also a prominent racehorse owner. With his wife Madeleine Damster, he resided at Red Court Villa on Hassan Sabry (ex-Gabalaya) street. They moved to Villa Lotus No. 20 Dar El Chefa Street, Garden City. (illegally pulled down in 1996 by the present owner which led to the firing of Cairo's deputy governor). In Switzerland, he resided at Chateau Neu-Habsburg (a medieval Habsburg fort) at Meggen. In the 1970s, Raoul and Simone Baehler sold the chateau to Switzerland's press baron, the Ringier family.

Baehler died in Switzerland on 12 September 1937 from post-operative complications. His sons, Rene and Gaston remained in Egypt. Rene, who cut a dashing figure with his spouse Aurore Souwaya on Cairo's dance floors, took over the Cosmopolitan Hotel. Rene is also remembered for having founded the Keigel Klub Kairo (KKK).

Les Grands Hotels d'Egypte

The George Nungovich Egyptian Hotels Co. was registered on February 24, 1899 as hotel proprietors. In 1921, the name of the company was changed to this title. The company owned the following hotels:
1. Continental-Savoy Hotel, in the centre of Cairo, built on land measuring 10,000 sq. metres.
2. Mena House Hotel, Pyramids, near Cairo.
3. Grand Hotel Helwan, at Helwan, near Cairo.
4. Tewfik Palace Hotel, at Helwan, near Cairo.
5. Hotel Casino San Stefano, Ramleh, Alexandria (since disposed of to Mr. Jack A. Barcilon for L.E. 145,000).

The first three hotels, excluding shop premises at the Continental-Savoy Hotel, have been leased to the Egyptian Hotels Ltd. until April 3, 1950 for a total annual rental of L.E. 35,150:
Continental Savoy Hotel L.E. 28,000
Mena House Hotel with Annexe L.E. 6,150
Grand Hotel Helwan L.E.1,000
The Tewfik Palace Hotel, Helwan, leased to the Ministry of Education for L.E. 1,280 a year.

Head Office: Continental-Savoy Hotel, Cairo.

Capital:
L.E. 144,300 divided into 37,000 Ordinary shares of £4 each, fully paid.

1 ACTION

١ سهم

Titre N° 08694 سند رقم

فنادق مصر الكبرى

شركة مساهمة مصرية

شركة چورج نيجوفيتش للفنادق المصرية سابقا

مصرح بها بمرسوم بتاريخ ٢٤ فبراير سنة ١٨٩٩

LES GRANDS HOTELS D'EGYPTE

SOCIÉTÉ ANONYME EGYPTIENNE

(anc. The George Nungovich Egyptian Hotels Company)

AUTORISÉE PAR DÉCRET EN DATE DU 24 FÉVRIER 1899

Siége Social : Le Caire — المركز الرئيسي القاهرة

رأس مالها ٢٩٦٠٠٠ جنيه مصري

مقسم الى ٧٤٠٠٠ سهم قيمة السهم الواحد اربعة جنيها مصريا مدفوعة باكملها

CAPITAL SOCIAL L.E. 296.000

DIVISÉ EN 74.000 ACTIONS DE LIVRES EGYPTIENNES QUATRE CHACUNE ENTIÈREMENT LIBÉRÉES

TITRE AU PORTEUR DE

UNE ACTION

DE L.EG. QUATRE

ENTIÈREMENT LIBÉRÉE

سند لحامله

بسهم واحد

قيمة أربعة جنيهات مصرية

دفعت بأكملها

N° 38134

UN ADMINISTRATEUR — عضو مجلس الادارة — UN ADMINISTRATEUR — عضو مجلس الادارة

LES GRANDS HOTELS D'EGYPTE — فنادق مصر الكبرى — S.A.E.

Le Caire, Février 1955. — القاهرة فى فبراير سنة ١٩٥٥

L.Eg. 4

٤ جنيه مصري

An American-designed bridge versus a Belgian-run tramway

Not only did its designer not jump from the it, but contrary to local parable, the landmark Abou al-Ela Bridge that once linked Gezira Island to Boulac opened weekdays for Nile traffic from 12:00 to 12:45 and again from 15:00 to 15:45.

The ornate, span-type metal Boulac Bridge — subsequently renamed Fouad Bridge and later Abou al-Ela — did however stop functioning several years after its inauguration, but that had more to do with lack of proper maintenance rather than faulty engineering.

As for the romanticized legend which claims Alexander-Gustave Eiffel (1832-1923) designed this bridge and later took his own life when it failed to open — not true.

This landmark Nile crossing is credited to American engineer William Donald Scherzer. Not only did his Chicago firm design the Boulac Bridge, but it was Scherzer who invented its ingenious rolling (bascules) and locking mechanism used for opening it to fluvial traffic. As for the bridge's French connection, that was limited to the manufacturing of steel girders by the well-known company of Five-Lilles, and to the steel beams produced by the famous French conglomerate Schneider.

But who financed this the 274.5 m. long and 20 m. wide bridge and why?

During the opening years of the 19th century, Cairo underwent an unprecedented real estate boom. It seemed that every month brought on a new urban development or suburb: Heliopolis, Dokki, Maadi, Garden City and Koubeh Gardens among them.

A group of Belgio-Swiss investors had similar plans for the island of Zamalek. In fact they had just completed a blueprint for its urbanization in anticipation of turning it into an attractive high-end suburb.

But before anything could be done, the island needed a second access bridge since the old and narrow Kasr al-Nil crossing had reached its maximum capacity. And since the proposed bridge had to open at given hours of the day enabling the smooth running of fluvial traffic, this meant 500 volts would be needed to operate its opening mechanism. Of the lift type, it would take two minutes for the bridge's two central movable spans to roll back on their wheels into a vertical position, thus allowing the waiting Nile traffic to sail through a 27 m. wide opening.

The money would be raised by local Belgian capitalists and the required electricity would be supplied by the nearby Tramway Power Plant in Boulac. In exchange, the Belgian-owned Societe Anonyme des Tramway du Caire would extend a tramway line across the proposed bridge, bisecting Zamalek as it sped towards Giza passing by the Zoo before linking up with the older Pyramids tramway line. And for an added bonus to the island, a special side track would be laid at the Zamalek side of the Boulac bringing the tramway right up to the Khedivial Sporting Club (today Gezira Club).

Société Anonyme des Tramways du Caire

Registered in Belgium on March 19, 1895 to acquire from the Société Generale des Chemins de Fer Economiques and Baron Edouard Empain the concession, originally fixed for 52 years and extended in 1908 until June 30, 1978. At the end of the concession, all the lines, rolling stock and depots would revert to the Government without compensation.

The Cairo tramways system comprised (in 1951) 70 kms. of double track, divided into 17 routes. The tramway centre was at Mohamed Aly Square (formerly Ataba el-Khadra).

The company used power for its system from the Société Egyptienne d'Electricité in which it held an important interest. It was also associated with the Egyptian General Omnibus Co. operating motor-bus services in Cairo.

Head Office: 1 Place du Trone, Brussels, Belgium.

Cairo Office: 1 Maspero Street (Boulac), Cairo.

Capital:
Belgian Fr 125,000,000 divided into 567,000 Parts Sociales of no par value.

SOCIÉTÉ ANONYME DES

TRAMWAYS DU CAIRE

SIÈGE SOCIAL : BRUXELLES

Constituée par acte authentique passé
devant Mr Charles P.-M. Van Halteren, notaire à Bruxelles, le 19 mars 1895
(Moniteur belge du 3 avril 1895) et dont les statuts ont été modifiés par décisions des Assemblées génér.ales du 2 juillet 1895
(Moniteur belge du 14 juillet 1895), du 20 octobre 1897 et de l'acte authentique de constatation du 22 mars 1898
(Moniteur belge des 31 octobre 1897 et 4-5 avril 1898),
du 11 novembre 1902 (Moniteur belge du 28 novembre 1902), du 19 octobre 1904 (Moniteur b.ge des 5, 17 et 20 novembre 19..
du 17 décembre 1904 (Moniteur belge du 4 janvier 1905), du 20 juin 1905 et de l'acte authentique de constatation du 22 janvier 19..
(Moniteur belge des 10-11 juillet 1905 et 8 février 1906), du 18 octobre 1905 (Moniteur belge du 29 octobre 1905,
du 19 avril 1907 et de l'acte authentique de constatation du 10 mars 1909 (Moniteur b.ge des 8 mai 1907 et 22-23 mars 1909),
du 13 janvier 1926 (Moniteur belge du 4 février 1926) et du 8 février 1927 Moniteur belge du 23 février 1927).

CAPITAL SOCIAL: 54,000,000 DE FRANCS

REPRÉSENTÉ PAR 540.000 PARTS SOCIALES SANS DÉSIGNATION DE VALEUR

PART SOCIALE SANS DÉSIGNATION DE VALEUR

UN ADMINISTRATEUR

No 433299

UN ADMINISTRATEUR

Bruxelles, le 1er mars 1927.

J. VERSCHUEREN - ANVERS-BRUXELLES

Dessin déposé

Erecting the new bridge was no easy feat. Construction took three and a half years with the foundations laid at 18 metres below sea level (33 m. below Nile level). In the pre-High Dam days, the portion of the Nile that ran through Egypt was a potent body of moving water, its strong currents and giant swirls, especially during high flood, causing serious challenges to bridge constructors. Several piers, large girders and wide spans had to be put in place before the bridge could be opened for business.

Civil engineering having won the day, the bridge was completed in 1912. But in sharp contrast to the pomp and ceremony surrounding the inaugurations of Cairo's older bridges or the multiple celebrations at the opening of the Aswan and Qena Reservoirs, when the Khedive and his guest, the Duke of Connaught, attended, the Boulac Bridge was very quietly opened to the public in July.

Summers in Cairo were hot and the entire government had moved to Alexandria the previous April. Khedive Abbas Hilmi II (r. 1892-1914) was summering in Europe with his Hungarian wife and Lord Kitchener, Egypt's de facto ruler, was attending an important meeting in Malta. It was therefore left to Ismail Sirry Pasha, the Minister of Public Works, to cut the ribbon on their behalf.

A month later, on 18 August 1912, Cairo's press corps was entertained to a magnificent champagne breakfast buffet at the Giza tramway station courtesy of Fritz de Lancker, the director of the Cairo Tramways Company. Together, they celebrated the launch of the new Ataba al-Khadra–Pyramids tram Route No. 3 by way of the new Boulac and Zamalek bridges.

Planned or not, that part of Zamalek traversed by tram Route No. 3 was owned by the Egyptian Hotels Company, itself controlled by the above mentioned Belgo-Swiss developers headed by the Swiss hotelier Charles Baehler. The company also owned the Gezira Palace Hotel (today, Marriott) whose parks and gardens covered most of Gezira-Zamalek's central area. The arrival of the tramway was understandably a roll-over prize.

The Anglo-Belgian Company of Egypt

Registered in England on March 3, 1906, to carry out general land and investment business. With land in Giza and Old Cairo suitable for building purposes, factory sites, etc. Sales of land were made on easy terms of payment, and loans were granted to buyers intending to erect dwelling-houses.

In 1906, having acquired the majority of shares of the Fayoum Light Railways Co., it assumed control. Following the reorganization of this railway in 1939, which involved the transfer of a big block of shares by the Anglo-Belgian Company, the shareholding of the Fayoum Light Railways was reduced to 10,701 shares out of the total of 24,305.

Head Office: Immobilia Building, 26 Cherif Pasha Street., Cairo.

Capital:
Intitial share capital was £348,340 in 69,668 Ordinary shares of £5 each, issued at £5.5s. During the years 1907-8 and 1909-10 capital was reduced to £345,690 by cancelling 530 shares. In 1925-26, as a result of accumulated losses amounting to £168,427, shareholders approved the reduction of capital from £345,690 to £172,845 by cancelling £2.5s. on each £5 share. Eventually, capital was increased to £211,907 in 1932-33 and to £219,657 in 1934-35.

5 5

Anglo-Belgian Company of Egypt
Limited.

Incorporated under the Companies Acts, 1862 to 1900.

Nº

CAPITAL £1,000,000

DIVIDED INTO

400,000 SHARES OF £2.10.0 EACH.

SHARE WARRANT TO BEARER FOR 5 SHARES OF TWO POUNDS TEN SHILLINGS

TITRE AU PORTEUR DE 5 ACTIONS DE £2.10.0 STERLING

Nos.

This is to Certify *that the Bearer of this Warrant is the Proprietor of* **FIVE** *fully paid up Shares numbered as above in the Capital of the* ANGLO-BELGIAN COMPANY OF EGYPT LIMITED *subject to the Articles of Association and other Regulations of the Company.*

Le porteur du present Titre *est Propriétaire de* **CINQ** *Actions entièrement libérées de l'* ANGLO-BELGIAN COMPANY OF EGYPT LIMITED, *portant les numéros indiqués ci-dessus et soumises aux conditions stipulées dans les Statuts et autres Réglements de la Compagnie*

GIVEN *under the Common Seal of the Company this*

SECRETARY.

DIRECTORS. ADMINISTRATEURS.

The Belgians of Egypt

Mention Belgians in Cairo and you'll automatically hear the words 'tramways' and 'Heliopolis' and by association 'Hindu folly' and 'Baron Empain'.

Heliopolis, of course, refers to the city by the same name created in 1906-7 by Baron Edouard Empain. During the project's dream-up phase, the city-to-be was also known as The Oasis. At least that is how it was described in the 1906 prospectus put out by its Belgian developers who had incorporated themselves into The Cairo Electric Railways & Heliopolis Oases Company. The new company's share issue was oversubscribed even before the first stone was laid in the desert, nine kilometres north of Cairo.

Hindu folly refers to Empain's palace on the airport road (ex Avenue des Palais, renamed Orouba Avenue in reference to the rising Pan Arabism under Nasser). Designed by French architect Alexandre Marcel (1860-1928) and decorated by Georges-Louis Claude (1879-1963), the Palais Hindou was completed in 1911.

Like other foreign resident communities in the 19th and the first half of the 20th century, the few Belgians who came to Egypt played a disproportionately important role in Egypt's cultural, economic and industrial development. These were a small, tight-knit community that kept a relatively low profile. And despite their more numerous and vociferous Gallic cousins, they nevertheless had friends in high places.

It was no secret that Sultan Hussein Kamel was an admirer of Baron Edouard Empain's enterprising spirit and, as though to prove it, had moved his family into the forty-room pseudo-oriental palazzo situated diagonally opposite the Hindu Palace, becoming the first Egyptian ruler to live in Heliopolis.

Against a colonial backdrop where Egypt was a virtual British crown territory, it was uphill for many of the Belgians who had invested in Egypt. Denied a board seat on the powerful British-run National Bank of Egypt, Baron Empain's successors in Egypt decided to launch a bank of their own. Although the Banque Belge et Internationale en Égypte was constituted on 30 January 1929 with a declared capital of one million Egyptian pounds, in reality it had replaced the older Banque Belge pour l'Etranger, which itself had taken over the portfolio of the Banque Sino-Belge's Egyptian branch. The earlier colonial bank's Cairo office was located at Kenissah al-Gedidah Street with sister branches in London, Peking (now Beijing), Shanghai and Tientsin.

The presence of a Belgian bank in Egypt lies in the on-going competition at the time between two of the world's most powerful trading and industrial groups. On one side of the English Channel, London was responsible for most of the global map being colored pink. On the other, were the Franco-Belgian conglomerates of which the Empain Group was an important composite.

The competition between these titans was mirrored in the Egyptian market by the battle of wills between Baron Empain's business concerns and those of his British nemesis, Sir Ernest Cassel, the chief backer of the Anglo-

Fayoum Light Railways Company

From Fayoum, reached by a branch line from Wasta Junction on the State Railway System, seven separate lines of 75 cm gauge radiated to Gharak, Shawashna, Agamine, Kalamsha, Lahoun, Sennoures and Rodah. Including sidings, they had a total working length of 168 kms. Construction commenced in 1898 by private enterprise under a concession granted by the Egyptian Government for seventy years expiring on August 15, 1972. At expiration of the term, the whole rights of the concessionaries revert, without compensation, to the Government that also had the option to purchase at any time after April 1945 with certain terms. In 1906, the Anglo-Belgian Company of Egypt Limited, having acquired the majority of the shares, assumed control.

In 1939, Joseph Kfoury, who operated a number of motor-bus services in Fayoum, acquired an important interest in the Fayoum Light Railways and was appointed managing director.

A motor-bus and lorry service in conjunction with the railway were inaugurated on October 24, 1935.

Capital:
£97,220 divided into 24,305 Ordinary shares of £4 each, fully paid.
1,795 Jouissance shares of no par value.
10,000 Founders shares of no par value.

FAYOUM

Light Railways Company

شركة السكك الحديديه الزراعيه بالفيوم

SOCIÉTÉ ANONYME

Authorized by a KHEDIVIAL DECREE dated 17th February 1898
and published in the "Journal Officiel" N°21 of Saturday 19th February 1898.

OFFICES OF THE COMPANY, CAIRO

Capital: £180,000 Sterling

DIVIDED INTO 22,500 SHARES OF £4 STERLING EACH
(pursuant to a resolution of the General Meeting in accordance with Art.5 of the Articles of Association)
AND 4,500 DEBENTURES OF £20 STERLING EACH

DEBENTURE TO BEARER FOR £20 STERLING

BEARING INTEREST AT 4% PER ANNUM

N° 2325

Cairo, 1st October 1899

FOR THE BOARD

DIRECTOR DIRECTOR

Judeo financial, commercial and industrial institutions in Egypt. For almost two decades these two men controlled directly or indirectly a significant portion of Egypt's commercial activities.

Although the highly visible Banque Belge directors: Pierre and Emanuel Bonvoisin, Louis van Damme, Jacques, Ellsworth Lambiotte and Robert Halet were relative latecomers on the scene, they were also the first to leave Egypt. Their precipitated departure was brought on by the assassination of Patrice Lumumba in the former Belgian Congo in February 1961. As though on queue, the Belgian Embassy in Cairo was ransacked and torched and all Belgian property seized.

When Belgian citizens were asked to leave on February 27 of that year, a unique chapter in Egypto-Belgian relations ended in bitter recriminations. Africa was in the process of de-colonization and the Arab World was closing ranks with its Third World brethren. No more White Man colonialism.

But it was precisely during the latter part of the colonialist era that foreign capital, foreign entrepreneurs and foreign labor found their way into Egypt. All the right economic indicators had been put in place, from an accommodating Khedive towing the British line, to a regime of Capitulations and Mixed Courts protecting foreign investors from local laws and taxes. It was open season for opportunity-seeking foreigners.

Even before Britain occupied Egypt, Belgian consuls during the reign of Mohammed Ali had established economic footholds in the port city of Alexandria. One of their first priorities was hiring a local dragoman or Mr. Fix-it who could facilitate the consul's entree into the Khedivial entourage for it was there that big contracts and lucrative commissions were handed out.

The dragoman (translator) was indispensable in any foreign legation or diplomatic agency. In the Arabic-speaking Middle East, dragomen were usually Greeks, Italians or local Christians with a basic European education.

In the case of the Belgians, a Syrian dragoman was hired by the name of Hanna Eid (Hanna afterwards gallicized to Jean). He spoke acceptable French, courtesy of one of the many missionary schools that spread French culture and ideals across the Levant. Eid would eventually found a mini-dragoman dynasty and, with time, was well connected to an ever-expanding network of diligent Syrian migrants who spread themselves across the Delta's cash-crop gathering centers.

Much later in the 19th century, the Belgians hitched a much more gratifying ride, this time with Armenian businessman-politician Boghos Nubar Pasha, son of Egypt's five-time Prime Minister Nubar Nubarian, confidante to two viceroys and three khedives. Had it not been for Boghos Nubar, there would never have been a Heliopolis.

In return for, and in proportion to, their services the Eids and the Nubars were amply compensated in money and in kind. These local beneficiaries brought into the game their respective cliques — the Khouris, Bicharas, Karams, Baharis (Syrians); and Artins, Arakels (Armenians) — all of whom became Belgian proteges and later claimed that country's citizenship. They were invariably referred to by their benefactors as *les faux Belges*.

Cie Immobiliere d'Égypte

A Belgian entreprenenial company founded in Cairo on April 7, 1900. It remained active in Cairo until its liquidation in 1935.

Its capital of FF 300,000 was divided in 12,000 shares of FF 250 each, in addition to 6,000 Founders' shares with no par value.

O. COLS

Nº 1758

Cie IMMOBILIÈRE D'EGYPTE
Sté ANONYME.

AUTORISÉE PAR DÉCRET KHÉDIVIAL DU 1er AVRIL 1900. LES STATUTS ONT ÉTÉ PUBLIÉS AU JOURNAL OFFICIEL D'ÉGYPTE DU 7 AVRIL 1900 ET AU MONITEUR BELGE DU 16-17 JUILLET 1900.

Siège Social, LE CAIRE.

CAPITAL SOCIAL 3,000,000 Frs.

REPRÉSENTÉ PAR 12,000 ACTIONS DE 250 Frs CHACUNE.

IL EST EN OUTRE CRÉÉ 6,000 PARTS DE FONDATEUR AU PORTEUR SANS DÉSIGNATION DE VALEUR.

PART DE FONDATEUR

AU PORTEUR.

UN ADMINISTRATEUR. L. Dutois

UN ADMINISTRATEUR.

Cie IMMOBILIÈRE D'EGYPTE (Sté ANONYME.)

TALON DE LA PART DE FONDATEUR Nº 1758

Contre remise du présent talon il sera délivré une nouvelle feuille de Coupons.

As the Eids and Nubars looked after Belgian affairs along with their own commercial interests, more Belgians arrived on the scene. Together, they created a handful of Belgian enterprises and joint ventures that would have an inversely proportional impact on Egypt's commercial development and infrastructure.

In the agricultural sector the most important companies set up with Belgian participation were the Gharbieh Land Co., the Kafr al-Dawar Co., the Agri-Industrial Co. and the Anglo-Belgian Company of Egypt.

In the industrial sector, one must evoke the two breweries (the Stella brand name became internationally known): The Crown Brewery of Alexandria and the Societe Anonyme Bieres Bomonti et Pyramides in Cairo.

In the financial sector there was the Mortgage Company of Egypt, and the Societe Generale Egyptienne pour l'Agriculture et le Commerce.

And there was of-course the all-powerful Banque Belge.

But it was in urban development that Belgians scored highest, particularly in the building and transport sectors. Belgian companies dealing in these sectors were the Societe Belge-Egyptienne de l'Ezbekieh, the Cairo Suburban Buildings Land Co. Ltd., The Koubbeh Gardens Co., and the Compagnie Immobiliere d'Égypte. There were also the construction giants of M. Padova, Leon Rolin & Co. inventors of the compressol system, and the Societe des Travaux Publics du Caire.

Most important among the Belgian transport companies was Empain's Cairo Electric Railways and Heliopolis Oases Company Limited followed by the Chemins de Fer de la Basse Egypte, the Fayoum Light Railways, the Tramways du Caire, the Tramways d'Alexandrie, Wagons Lits & Grands Express Europeens, and the Menzaleh Canal and Navigation Co.

There were also those enterprising individuals who penetrated the inner sanctum of the Khedivial court. The Carton de Wiart brothers are a good example. One brother, Rene , was an officer in the Khedivial household, the other, Maitre Leon Carton de Wiart, was a well-known court magistrate. The de Wiarts benefited from a direct pipeline to King Leopold in Brussels through their cousin Edmond Carton de Wiart. This fortuitous occurrence helped the de Wiart brothers to circumvent the often long and expensive middleman route. They were also instrumental in laying the groundwork for the King of the Belgian's visit to Egypt in 1930.

Just as the de Wiart brothers were about to retire from the local scene, the Eeman family, George, Ernest and Jacques, came of professional age. The last two were learned judges at the Mixed Courts to whom the legal jargon was deja vu since Egypt's Constitution of 1923 was modeled on its Belgium counterpart. Another sharp legal mind that made it to the top of Egypt's judiciary was Maurice de Wee, one of the last presidents of the Mixed Courts which wrapped up its activities in 1949, when Egypt's judicature became the only law of the land.

Somewhere between the de Wiarts and the abolition of the Capitulations was the adept jurist Maurice Jacquet,

The Electric Light and Power Supply Co.

The Electric Light and Power Supply Co. was registered on July 3, 1906. The company owned a 40-year concession from the Daira Khassa of the ex-Khedive Ismail for supplying electric current to Ezbekia quarter of Cairo, an important shopping and amusement district. The concession expired on March 19, 1946. The company, however, was authorized to continue its activities until the end of December, 1948.

Office: 13 Bustan el-Dekka St, Cairo.

Capital: L.E. 36,000 divided into 9,000 Jouissance shares of no par value.
Share capital was L.E. 36,000 divided into 9,000 Capital shares of L.E. 4 each. The shares were redeemed progressively out of profits and converted into Jouissance shares.

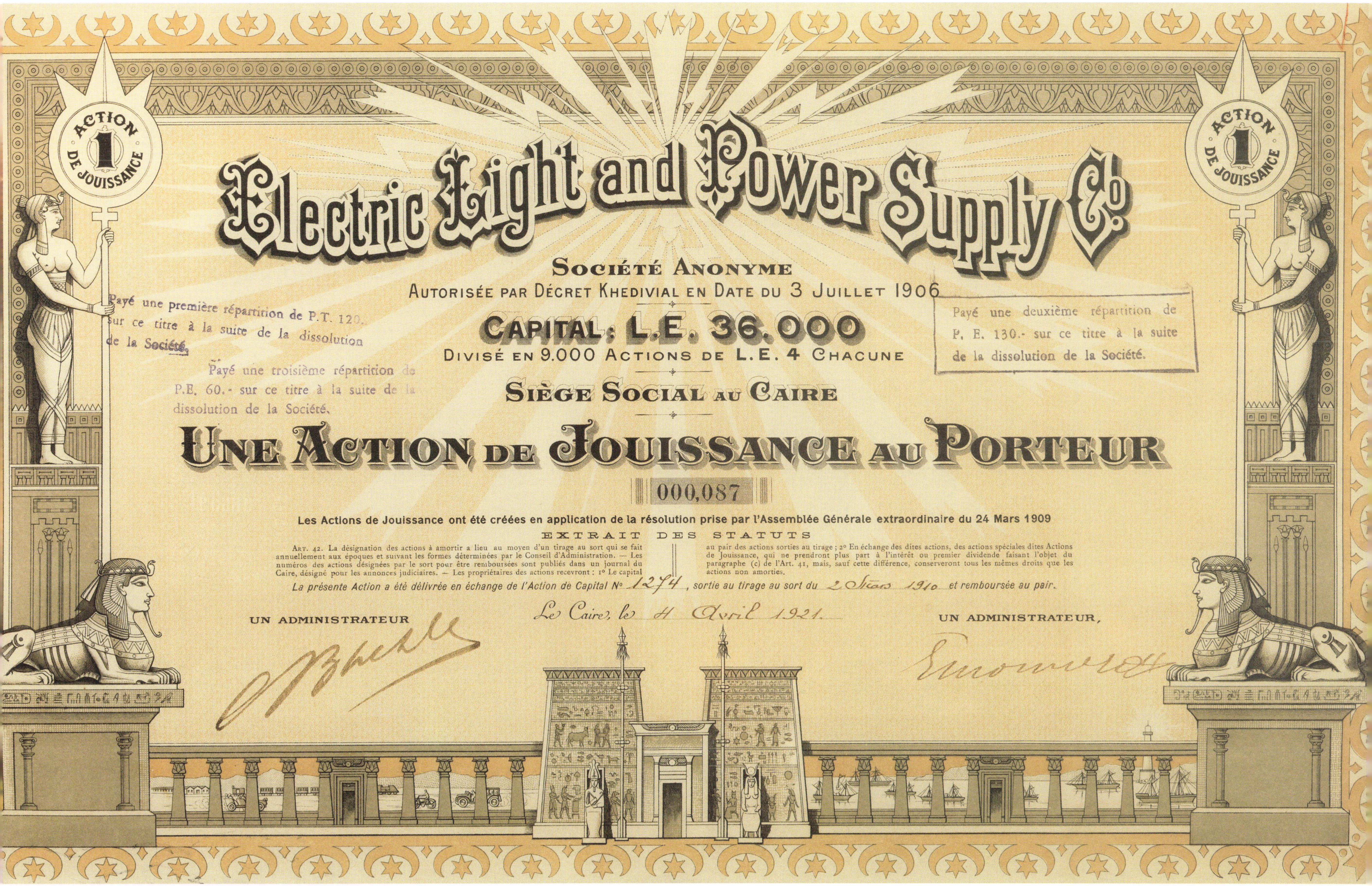

ACTION 1 DE JOUISSANCE

ACTION 1 DE JOUISSANCE

Electric Light and Power Supply Co

Société Anonyme

Autorisée par Décret Khedivial en Date du 3 Juillet 1906

CAPITAL : L.E. 36.000

Divisé en 9.000 Actions de L.E. 4 Chacune

Siège Social au Caire

Payé une première répartition de P.T. 120. sur ce titre à la suite de la dissolution de la Société.

Payé une deuxième répartition de P. E. 130.- sur ce titre à la suite de la dissolution de la Société.

Payé une troisième répartition de P.E. 60.- sur ce titre à la suite de la dissolution de la Société.

Une Action de Jouissance au Porteur

000,087

Les Actions de Jouissance ont été créées en application de la résolution prise par l'Assemblée Générale extraordinaire du 24 Mars 1909

EXTRAIT DES STATUTS

Art. 42. La désignation des actions à amortir a lieu au moyen d'un tirage au sort qui se fait annuellement aux époques et suivant les formes déterminées par le Conseil d'Administration. — Les numéros des actions désignées par le sort pour être remboursées sont publiés dans un journal du Caire, désigné pour les annonces judiciaires. — Les propriétaires des actions recevront : 1° Le capital au pair des actions sorties au tirage ; 2° En échange des dites actions, des actions spéciales dites Actions de Jouissance, qui ne prendront plus part à l'intérêt ou premier dividende faisant l'objet du paragraphe (c) de l'Art. 41, mais, sauf cette différence, conserveront tous les mêmes droits que les actions non amorties.

La présente Action a été délivrée en échange de l'Action de Capital N° 1274, sortie au tirage au sort du 2 Mars 1910 et remboursée au pair.

Le Caire, le 4 Avril 1921.

UN ADMINISTRATEUR

UN ADMINISTRATEUR,

King Fouad's trusted legal counsel. In 1937, Jacquet was among the Egyptian delegation to the Montreux Conference which negotiated the end of the Mixed Courts regime. Later during, the Second World War, Jacquet (seconded by Emile Jacobs) headed the 'rebel' Belgian Union in Egypt. This was the darkest hour of the small Belgian community in Egypt which had spilt into two opposing factions: those loyal to King Leopold, now reduced to a nominal ruler of occupied Belgium, and those like Jacquet who stood firmly behind Britain and its allies.

Although the Belgian captains and kings of Egyptian industry looked to Edouard Empain as the honorary doyen of Egypt's Belgian community, it was to Henri Naus Bey (1875-1938), to whom they turned for advice.

Naus Bey and Anne Etty, his Javanese-raised wife, came to Egypt at the turn of the century. With the assistance of his two proteges, Albert Ceyssens and Raoul Roche, Naus successfully reorganized the Egyptian Sugar Company which had suffered a coup de grace when its chairman Ernest Cronier committed suicide in Paris after loosing much of the company's assets at the Paris Bourse. Under the Naus administration, the Sucreries flourished becoming the standard banner for all other agro-industrial projects. Although the Societe des Sucreries et Rafineries d'Égypte started out as a Franco-Jewish consortium (Cronier-Suarès), for several decades after it was run exclusively by Belgians.

Naus developed a close relationship with Egypt's King Fouad and it was at the latter's prompting that he sat on numerous business and charity boards. Henri Naus created the Assistance Publique (ambulance) of Egypt in 1910 and was its first vice-president and later its president. He was also treasurer of the Red Crescent of Egypt.

In 1922, Naus was nominated the first President of the Egyptian Federation of Industries, a very prestigious and influential position at the time.

Belgians contributed to Egypt's tourist industry. An entire generation of Egypt's international café society are in their debt of Joe Renson, Marcel Herman and Paul Delcave — the famous hoteliers who took turns at the helm of the Hotels Company of Egypt and helped launch the famous Semiramis Hotel's Grill Room and its legendary Roof Garden. Both outlets were immortalized in many books dealing with Egypt's belle epoque.

It was also thanks to Egypt's Belgian clique that the matchless Heliopolis Palace Hotel came into being in the early teens of this century. Its designer was Belgian architect Ernest Jaspar.

The Belgians who had come to Egypt in late 19th century and early 20th gave a new meaning to the words international cooperation. They lived well in Egypt and gave generously in return.

Crown Brewery

The Crown Brewery was registered in Belgium on May 15, 1897 as brewers and ice and mineral water manufacturers. It has a selling agreement, with the Bomonti Brewery for the sale of beer.

On May 5, 1945, the excise duty on beer was increased from P.T. 240 to P.T. 300 per hectoliter. This was the fourth increase since January 28, 1940. Prior to that, the rate was P.T. 60 per hectoliter. Local beer is about 97% water and 3% alcohol.

Beer brewed in Egypt was formerly dependent entirely upon imported raw materials. But proprietors of local breweries created a local malting industry, put up the necessary installations at Giza, near Cairo, and turned thousands of ardebs of Egyptian barley into malt.

Head Office: Brussels, Belgium.

Brewery: 39 Eleusis Street (Ibrahimieh), Ramleh, Alexandria.

Capital:
E.F. 3,200,000 (L.E. 123,440) divided into 32,000 Ordinary shares of E.F. 100 each, fully paid.

CROWN BREWERY

SOCIÉTÉ ANONYME

Constituée par acte passé devant Mᵉ **ECTORS**, *notaire à Bruxelles, le 15 mai 1897; modifications aux statuts suivant actes passés devant Mᵉ* **ECTORS**, *notaire à Bruxelles, les 1ᵉʳ octobre 1898, 5 avril 1899, 22 juillet 1913, 22 septembre 1913, 14 février et 6 mars 1920, et devant Mᵉ* **OVERLEAUX-LAGASSE**, *notaire à Bruxelles, le 4 juin 1907. Ces actes sont publiés au* MONITEUR BELGE *du 2 juin 1897 sous le nº 2269, des 10-11 octobre 1898 sous le nº 3826, du 21 avril 1899 sous le nº 1887, du 23 juin 1907 sous le nº 3804, des 13-14 août 1913 sous le nº 5838, du 8 octobre 1913 sous le nº 6879, des 8-9 mars 1920 sous le nº 2164, et du 19 mars 1920 sous le nº 2535.*

CAPITAL SOCIAL : 2,432,500 FRANCS

Entièrement versé et représenté par 24,325 actions de capital de 100 francs chacune

Il a été créé en outre 5,650 actions de jouissance sans désignation de valeur

Action de Capital de 100 fr. au Porteur

ENTIÈREMENT LIBÉRÉE

Nº 22,144

faisant partie des neuf mille trois cent vingt-cinq actions de capital créées par l'assemblée générale extraordinaire du 14 février 1920 en représentation d'une augmentation de capital résultant de l'affectation du fonds de prévision à concurrence de 932,500 francs, à la dite augmentation.

Cette action ne peut être négociée que dix jours après la publication du bilan de l'exercice 1921, jusqu'à cette époque, elle ne peut être cédée que suivant le mode prévu par l'art. 47, al. 2, de la loi sur les sociétés.

Bruxelles, le 6 mars 1920.

Un Administrateur, | Un Administrateur,

Imp. et lith. de la Cour, L. VAN DER AA, 7 rue de la Cuiller, Bruxelles. — Tél. Br. 32.40. — 371-20

Stella's grandpa

Even the most abstaining teetotaler has heard of the golden liquid in the green bottle sporting the yellow label and blue star. La blonde Stella, Egypt's leading beer, has been called for almost a century, survived a whopping recession, two world wars, a coup d'etat, sequestration and, more recently, a spate of religious conservatism.

The older generations may still remember how, if arak was not available, the affordable Stella (6.5 piasters a bottle in the 1940s) always took precedence at the Kit-Kat, the Dahabia, the Parisienne, Chez Badia or Casino al-Shagara. Not a Christmas or Shabatt passed where Stella was not present on the table whenever guests appeared. Sham al-Nessim would invariably mean *fessikh* with Stella. Some old timers argue that it was thanks to Stella that the Aussies and Kiwis defeated the Pils-drinking Krauts at Alamein.

Incorporated in Belgium, home to the world famous Stella Artois, the first producers of the Egyptian Stella opened shop in May 1898 under the name of the Crown Brewery Company of Cairo. But to avoid confusion with its older Alexandria sibling by the same name, the directors quickly decided on a name change: Société Anonyme Brasserie des Pyramides (Pyramids Brewery). For several decades thereafter, the fortress-like beer plant in the district of Bein al-Sarayat remained one Giza's most famous landmarks. Fortunately, the plant is still with us today.

Pyramids Brewery's first public share offering comprised 15,000 shares priced at FF 100 each. Due to high start-up costs, the company was obliged to launch a second share issue in November 1904 bringing total shares on the market to 20,000. But with careful investments and the combination of Belgian know-how and equipage, Pyramids Brewery gradually displaced existing mom n' pop beer manufacturers and stood up to famous imported brand names including Bremen's Burton Beck & Co. and the widespread Guinness Stout.

At first, treated Nile water was used for the production of the golden ale, but finding it was not up to the required standard, Pyramids Brewery resorted to aquifers. Another change in keeping with growing demand was the necessity to keep a constant stock of 6,281 hectoliters with a guaranteed four-month storage period to ensure quality. All these changes came with a hefty price tag, yet by year-end 1906, Pyramids Brewery made it into the black showing a profit of FF 164,023 with a 30% increase in overall production. Board chairman Joseph G. Chakour Pasha could now toast his fellow directors Messrs. L. Carton de Wiart, Florent Lambert, J. Debonne, Alfonso Colucci and L. Dumonceau. And with 34 brasseries and beer halls already registered in Cairo, there would be many more toasts to come.

In Alexandria, beer drinkers were more than satisfied with their own local brew. They had a choice between an ale produced by the Swiss Bomonti Brothers of Karmous, near Alexandria's Mahmoudia Canal, or that marketed by the Alexandria Crown Brewery Company launched at Ibrahimieh in 1897.

It would take a series of mergers and acquisitions — the first in 1909 and the last on Christmas day 1922 — before the emerging Bomonti & Pyramids Beer Company could call itself Egypt's leading brewery. By then, Stella

Bieres Bomonti & Pyramides

The Societe Anonyme des Bieres Bomonti et Pyramides was registered on December 25, 1922 to acquire the activities of the Societe Anonyme Belge des Brasseries d'Egypte, then in liquidation. The acquisition was effected through the exchange of shares: 38,700 fully paid Bomonti and Pyramides shares exchanged for a similar number of Brasseries d'Egypte shares. The Societe Anonyme des Brasseries d'Egypte was originally established in 1909, following the acquisition of the Brasseries des Pyramides and the Brasserie et Rizrie Bomonti Freres.

The company is engaged in brewing beer, manufacturing malt, mineral waters and fruit drinks. The decortication and glazing of rice for export and local consumption is carried out on a large scale at the Alexandria factory. There was an agreement with the Crown Brewery of Alexandria for the sale of beer.

Head Office and Brewery: Sarwat Street, Dokki, Cairo.

Capital:
L.E. 192,875 divided into 50,000 Ordinary shares of E.Fc 10 each, fully paid.

1 OBLIGATION

SOCIÉTÉ ANONYME DES BIÈRES BOMONTI & PYRAMIDES · ALEXANDRIE EGYPTE

100 LIVRES EGYPTIENNES

Société Anonyme des Bières Bomonti & Pyramides

SOCIÉTÉ ANONYME EGYPTIENNE

AU CAPITAL DE CINQ MILLIONS DE FRANCS AU PAIR

Siège Social à Alexandrie

EMISSION DE 300 OBLIGATIONS À 5%

Faite en vertu de la décision de l'Assemblée Générale du 15 Avril 1937 et de la décision du Conseil d'Administration en date du 15 Avril 1937.

Obligation de 100 Livres Egyptiennes au Porteur

N° 102

SOCIÉTÉ ANONYME DES BIÈRES BOMONTI ET PYRAMIDES Alexandrie

rapportant 5% d'intérêt annuel, soit L.Eg. 5,- payable à raison de L.Eg. 2,500 mms le 30 Septembre et L.Eg. 2,500 mms le 31 Mars de chaque année à partir du 30 Septembre 1937.

Les 300 obligations sont remboursables par L.Eg. 100,- chacune en 16 ans à partir du 31 Mars 1942.

Le premier remboursement se fera le 30 Septembre 1942 conformément au tableau d'amortissement ci-contre.

L'obligation désignée pour être remboursée ne rapporte plus aucun intérêt depuis le jour où elle est remboursable.

Le montant total des obligations émises par la Société ne dépassera pas L.Eg. 50.000,-

Aucune hypothèque ne sera accordée par la Société à des tiers sur ses terrains et immeubles avant remboursement de ces obligations.

La Société se réserve le droit de rembourser au pair le montant non amorti à partir du 30 Septembre 1943.

Les obligations deviennent immédiatement remboursables de plein droit en cas d'infraction par la Société à l'un de ses engagements.

Alexandrie, le 15 Avril 1937.

UN ADMINISTRATEUR: H. Orm

UN ADMINISTRATEUR:

1 OBLIGATION

100 LIVRES EGYPTIENNES

TYPO-LITHO. FLLI. VENTURA, ALEX.

beer had become the symbol of reliability and good times. Things got even better when a million thirsty Allied soldiers passed through Egypt during WWII. By its fiftieth year, Stella beer had become an international brand name without ever leaving Egyptian soil.

After the war, with a capital of LE 192,875, Bomonti & Pyramids Beer Company underwent major changes in conformity with the New Company Act requiring larger Egyptian representation on company boards. This was when Cotton King Mohammed Ahmed Fargahli Pasha also became known as King Beer, as he became the first Egyptian to run Bomonti & Pyramids. About this time, the company entered into a technical-assistance agreement with Heineken.

In July 1953, a year after the hurried departure of another king — Farouk of Egypt — the Bomonti in the company's name was dropped and the Pyramids arabized to *al Ahram*. More changes came in 1962 when Ahram Beverages along with Egypt's entire private sector succumbed to sequestration and nationalization. Crown Brewery Company of Alexandria which had so far resisted merging with its Cairo nemesis, did so by ministerial decree. Competition and quality suffered as government appointees, free from shareholder accountability, were coerced into importing the company's needs from the Soviet Union and its Eastern satellites. The era of a flat, stingless Stella had arrived.

It was during this time that a non-alcoholic brand — Birell — was launched as a means of placating growing anti-secular sentiment calling for the summary prohibition of the golden ale. A compromise was found when alcoholic beverages were banned from non-touristic sites and during the month of Ramadan. But time was on Stella' s side. By successfully launching Egypt's first ever GDR financing in 1997, Ahram Beverages Company found itself at the center of media attention and at the vanguard of Egypt's move towards privatization. Despite those who had exaggerated Stella's demise, the golden froth is today the beacon of economic change. Another beer-making milestone achieved in time for Stella's 100th birthday.

Société de Bière "Les Pyramides"

Bieres Bomonti & Pyramides in its new form after July 1953.

5 ACTIONS

٥ أسهم

شركة بيرة الأهرام

شركة مساهمة مصرية

مصرح بها بمرسوم بتاريخ ٢٥ ديسمبر سنة ١٩٢٢ معدل بمرسوم بتاريخ ٢٢ يوليو سنة ١٩٥٣

SOCIÉTÉ DE BIÈRE "LES PYRAMIDES"

SOCIÉTÉ ANONYME EGYPTIENNE

AUTORISÉE PAR DÉCRET DU 25 DÉCEMBRE 1922

MODIFIÉ PAR DÉCRET DU 22 JUILLET 1953

رأس مالها ٣٠٠٠٠٠ جنيه مصري

بموجب جمعية عمومية غير عادية منعقدة بتاريخ ٢٧ فبراير سنة ١٩٥٦

وزع على ١٥٠٠٠٠ سهم قيمة السهم الواحد جنيهان مصريان

CAPITAL SOCIAL L.E. 300.000

EN VERTU D'UNE ASSEMBLÉE GÉNÉRALE EXTRAORDINAIRE EN DATE DU 27 FÉVRIER 1956

DIVISÉ EN 150.000 ACTIONS DE L.Eg. 2 CHACUNE

SIÈGE SOCIAL: GUIZEH (LE CAIRE) — المركز الرئيسي : بالجيزة (القاهرة)

SOCIÉTÉ DE BIÈRE "LES PYRAMIDES" S.A.E.

خمسة أسهم لحاملها

قيمة كل سهم جنيهان مصريان مدفوعة بكاملها

TITRE AU PORTEUR DE CINQ ACTIONS

DE L.E. DEUX CHACUNE – ENTIÈREMENT LIBÉRÉES

N° 22141 À N° 22145

احد اعضاء مجلس الادارة
UN ADMINISTRATEUR

Guizeh, Avril 1956
(Egypte)

الجيزة في ابريل سنة ١٩٥٦
(مصر)

احد اعضاء مجلس الادارة
UN ADMINISTRATEUR

L.Eg. 10

١٠ جنيهات مصرية

LITH. F^lli VENTURA ALEXANDRIE

Sednaoui

The odd man out among Cairo's department stores was Sednaoui. While most other stores belonged to Jews, the owners of Sednaoui were Nazarenes from the Syrian villages of Sednaya and Maaloula where Aramaic was spoken until very recently.

Newly arrived in Egypt by way of Damascus, the Sednaoui brothers, Samaan and Selim opened their first haberdashery in the late nineteenth century in the district of Hamzaoui before moving to Mousky Street in al-Azhar.

The brothers' fortune took a turn for the better when employees of the Khedivial harem had either overpaid or forgotten to take back the correct change. When Khawaga Samaan ran after them pointing out what happened, the much obliged shoppers returned to their palace and related their exceptional encounter with an honest Shami (Syrian). From that day onwards Sednaoui was a favorite among court ladies.

As Cairo expanded into the new European quarter of Ismailia, so did the city's great retailing names: Chemla, Cicurel and Ades were clustered on or near Avenue Fouad (today 26th of July), considered by many as Cairo's Oxford Street. Whereas Orosdi-Back (Omar Effendi) was within walking distance on Sharia Abdel Aziz, Tiring, Stein and Morums had already opened on Ataba Square, the nexus of Cairo's commercial hub.

The Sednaoui brothers kept their distance from the rest of the department stores setting up shop in the more confined Place Khazindar. It was there on 4 November 1913, in the presence of Prince Mohammed Ali Tewfik, that they inaugurated their grand three-story emporium near al-Bawaki, opposite the Services Club.

In no time, Sednaoui at Khazindar became the orgeuil of their retail chain with branches in Alexandria, Port Said, Tantah, Mansourah, Fayoum and Assiout. And in keeping with the time and a rising demand for their wares, the department store's flagship was considerably revamped and enlarged with much celebration taking place in May 1925 at the re-opening.

In view of its classical fin de siècle architecture, Sednaoui could have been transplanted from any one of the great European capitals. In his quest to emulate Galleries Lafayette on Boulevard Hausmann in Paris, architect George Parcq spared nothing in terms of layout, metalwork and general amenities. Even the flag flying cupolas were there. Yet it was no secret that Sednaoui played second fiddle to the high-end Cicurel.

While Cicurel set the trends of consumer culture in Cairo, Sednaoui was not far behind. If the handsome and formidably attired Tcherkess guards flanked Cicurel's grand entrance on Avenue Fouad, Cairo ladies were extremely flattered whenever Monsieur Sednaoui greeted them personally as they marched through the portals of his emporium — an enticing tactic he did fairly regularly.

The clever merchant-turned-Bey and later Papal Count in view of his extensive charities, promoted the idea that

Société Selim et Samaan Sednaoui

Founded in 1878 as Selim and Samaan Sednaoui, the original firm was converted into an English limited company on January 22, 1907. The company owns department stores in Cairo, Alexandria, Port Said, Tantah, Mansourah, Fayoum and Assiut.

Cairo Store and Head Office: Khazindar Square.

Alexandria Store: 1, Sidi Metwalli Street.

Capital: £645,000 divided into 6,45 Ordinary Shares of £100 each, fully paid.

شركة سليم وسمعان صيدناوي

شركة مساهمة متمتعة بجنسية الجمهورية العربية المتحدة

سجل تجارى رقم ٣٧٧ القاهرة

SOCIÉTÉ SELIM ET SAMAAN SEDNAOUI

SOCIÉTÉ ANONYME R.A.U.

R. C. Nº 377 - LE CAIRE

تأسست سنة ١٩٠٧

ورخص لها في الاستمرار في العمل كشركة مساهمة متمتعة بجنسية الجمهورية العربية المتحدة بموجب قرار رئيس الجمهورية رقم ٧٨ لسنة ١٩٥٩

رأس مال الشركة ٦٣٠٠٠٠ جنيه مصرى

موزع على ٦٣٠٠٠ سهم قيمة كل منها عشرة جنيهات مصرية

مركز الشركة الرئيسى بالقاهرة

ميدان الخازندار

خمسة وعشرون سهما اسميا

قيمة كل منها عشرة جنيهات مصرية

رقم ٠٠٣٦٢٢٦ الى ٠٠٣٦٢٥٠

عضو مجلس الادارة

عضو مجلس الادارة

اسم المساهم: السيد سليم الياس صيدناوي

القاهرة فى ١٢ يناير ١٩٥٩

25 ACTIONS NOMINATIVES L.E.10

٢٥ سهما اسميا قيمة كل منها عشرة جنيهات مصرية

any ordinary *sit* (woman) who bought from Sednaoui was automatically treated as a *hanem* (lady). Sednaoui recalled only too well how the enunciations of a woman could influence shopping habits city-wide.

Either Samaan Sednaoui or one of his heirs were always there before the store opened to the public, scanning the arrival of their well-mannered dandified male and female employees, inspecting them as they drifted to their stations. Once all was in shipshape, the store opened for business.

As they entered Sednaoui, shoppers were immediately taken in by the grandiose atrium. Once inside, they would gape at the jewelry and cosmetic counters while the more courageous would try out the latest Parisian hats and accessories. Men, too, stopped at Sednaoui's purchasing rolls of imported English cloth or Far Eastern fabrics for their wives or sweethearts.

Another unannounced advantage was how Sednaoui's quickly became the preferred lieu for a fleeting flirt because of its multiple entrances which formed perfect getaways for the faint-hearted.

And there was also the toy department where wide-eyed kiddies thought they had discovered heaven.

Masters of the retail universe, the Sednaouis made it seem like there was a special event each day of the year. And everything could be bought on account.

Through their extensive purchasing agents in Paris, London and New York and with the assistance of Sednaoui Shipping Co. Ltd. of Princess Street, Manchester (later, Selfridges, London), nothing was beyond Sednaoui's reach. Catalogues burst with seasonal buys whether for Christmas, Easter, Bairam or back-to-school.

There were also those popular annual low-end sales. These were anticipated by the modest and lower middle income shoppers who, intimidated by Cicurel's sophistication, showed up boldly at Place Khazindar armed with the one-page newspaper ad listing the various Sednaoui discounts. For some, it was their only exposure ever to an in-store fashion show, an auction, Santa Claus or Christmas in July.

For the big spenders, shopping at Sednaoui was more for pleasure than satisfying basic needs. On certain Sundays in the late 1950s, when the rest of commercial Cairo was shut down, Sednaoui opened by special arrangement to accommodate wealthy shop-till-you-drop clients from Saudi Arabia and the Gulf emirates. These arrived by the plane-load with an extra one in reserve for the fully laden return trip.

In July 1961, Egypt's major department stores were nationalized wholesale. Mr. Elie Sednaoui, the then-director of S&S Sednaoui et Fils, was given an indefinite leave of absence. An army officer had come to replace him.

The age of drab counters and khaki-colored cooperatives was about to begin.

Grands Magasins Chemla

The Grands Magasins Chemla were established in Egypt in 1907. On October 1, 1945, the partners of the firm decided to convert the undertaking into an Egyptian limited company. The company owns the largest department stores in Cairo.

Department Store and Offices: 11 Avenue Fouad I, Cairo.

Capital:
L.E. 400,000 divided into 100,00 Ordinary shares of L.E. 4 each, fully paid. The shares were last quoted at P.T. 473.

25 ACTIONS

٢٥

محلات شملا الكبرى

شركة مساهمة مصرية

GRANDS MAGASINS CHEMLA S.A.E.

SOCIÉTÉ ANONYME EGYPTIENNE
AUTORISÉE PAR DÉCRET ROYAL EN DATE DU 5 MAI 1946
PUBLIÉ AU JOURNAL OFFICIEL N° 52 DU 16 MAI 1946

صادر بتأسيسها مرسوم ملكي
بتاريخ ٥ مايو سنة ١٩٤٦ ونشر بالجريدة الرسمية
بالعدد نمرة ٥٢ بتاريخ ١٦ مايو سنة ١٩٤٦

CAPITAL L.E. 400,000

DIVISÉ EN 100.000 ACTIONS DE L.E. QUATRE
CHACUNE, ENTIÈREMENT VERSÉES

رأسمالها ٤٠٠٠٠٠ جنيه مصري
مقسمة الى ١٠٠٠٠٠ سهم قيمة كل سهم منها
أربعة جنيهات مصرية مدفوعة بأكملها

Titre de Vingt cinq Actions au porteur

مستند عن خمسة وعشرين سهما لحاملها

Actions No. 77151 à No. 77175 رقم

بنك مصر

UN ADMINISTRATEUR عضو مجلس الادارة

UN ADMINISTRATEUR عضو مجلس الادارة

LE CAIRE, LE 15 AOÛT 1946. القاهرة فى ١٥ أغسطس سنة ١٩٤٦

100 ج.م

١٠٠ جنيه مصري

WHITEHEAD MORRIS EGYPT

The ephemeral republic of Kom-Ombo

It was announced in London on Thursday, 6 October 1994, that Spink's, in association with Christie's of St. James, would hold the W. Benson Collection and other Banknote Auction.

"Nine hundred and eighty lots covering some of the world's oldest and rarest currencies are expected to be sold to the highest international bidders at Christie's Ryder Street rooms between 10:00 and 14:00."

Although its banknotes were not half as elegant or colorful as the rest, lot No. 567 was earmarked at 5,500 to 6,500 pounds sterling making it the most expensive of the entire collection. More perplexing is that the banknote didn't resemble any customary legal tender.

Spink's numismatic auction catalogue describes item No. 567 in the following terms:

"A series of Banknote from Wadi Kom-Ombo [a town in Upper Egypt] printed for use during April and May 1919 in the event of Kom-Ombo being cut off from the outside world by political unrest in the area. This set comprising 5-, 10- and 50- piasters and 1-, 5-, and 10- Livres believed to be the only set extant, the balance being recalled and replaced, except one set retained by the Wadi Kom-Ombo Company. All the notes are in plain script on card with semi-circular handstamp, SOCIETE ANONYME DE WADI KOM-OMBO. Script reads 'I am the inspector who signed at Kom-Ombo, pay to the bearer on demand'."

What is not mentioned anywhere in Spinks' catalogue, is that the notes described in lot No. 567 were signed by Ahmed Moustafa Bey (d. 1940), the veteran mufatish (inspector) and senator from the district of Kom-Ombo in Upper Egypt.

With the completion in 1902 of the Aswan Reservoir and its subsequent heightening in 1909, along with the digging of a network of irrigation canals, several hundred thousand feddans were brought under cultivation for the first time. The heretofore unknown abundance of water during the dry season allowed for perennial irrigation so that a second crop was planted each year.

These important developments led to a doubling of land value, the allocation of the new acreage to sugar cane and the burgeoning of sugar factories all over Upper Egypt. Sugar production would become the single largest industrial employer and sugar cane cultivation the nation's second largest cash crop.

This was a reversal from when Egypt's sugar industry had fallen on hard times, once during the reign of Mohammed Ali and again following the 28 August 1905 suicide of French sugar king Ernest Cronier.

Cronier, together with Henri Says & Cie of Paris and banker Raphael Suarès of Cairo, had re-launched Egypt's sugar industry in 1892. Thirteen years later, Cronier's failed speculation on the Paris Bourse led to his hastened demise and the insolvency of Egypt's sugar consortium.

Société Anonyme de Wadi Kom-Ombo

Registered on April 14, 1904 to develop and cultivate some 70,000 acres of desert land which it owned at Wadi Kom Ombo, Aswan Province, 500 miles south of Cairo.

The main crops raised were sugar-cane, wheat, maize, barley and beans. The sugar-cane yield was sold to the Société Generale des Sucrerie et de la Raffinerie d'Egypte and was crushed by that company in its factory specially erected in the Kom Ombo district to absorb the output of local plantations. The area of the property under cultivation in 1946 was approximately 30,000 feddans.

Head Office: Immobilia Building, 26 Cherif Pasha St., Cairo.

Capital:
1,800,000 divided into 450,000 Ordinary shares of £4 each, fully paid.
15,000 Founders shares of no par value.

SOCIÉTÉ ANONYME DE WADI KOM-OMBO

Autorisée par décret de S.A. le Khédive d'Egypte en date du 14 Avril 1904 publié avec les Statuts, au Journal Officiel du Gouvernement Egyptien du 18 Avril 1904, N°44 (supplément), et transcrit ainsi que lesdits Statuts, sur le registre des actes de société au greffe commercial du Tribunal mixte du Caire, le 25 du même mois, sub N° 68

1 ACTION

SIÈGE SOCIAL : AU CAIRE

Lst. 4

2ème ÉMISSION D'ACTIONS

ÉMISSION DE 75.000 ACTIONS DE LST. 4 CHACUNE, CRÉÉES PAR DÉCISION DU CONSEIL D'ADMINISTRATION EN DATE DU 24 NOVEMBRE 1905, EN VERTU D'UNE DÉLIBÉRATION DE L'ASSEMBLÉE GÉNÉRALE DES ACTIONNAIRES DU 10 AVRIL 1905

(PAR CETTE ÉMISSION, LE CAPITAL SOCIAL - QUI ÉTAIT DE LST. 300.000 ET DIVISÉ EN 75.000 ACTIONS DE LST. 4 CHACUNE SE TROUVE ÉLEVÉ A LST. 600.000 ET DIVISÉ EN 150.000 ACTIONS DE LST. 4 CHACUNE)

(LES TITRES DE CETTE SECONDE ÉMISSION SONT NUMÉROTÉS DE 19.001 À 38.000 ET LES ACTIONS DE 75.001 À 150.000)

TITRE N° 26327

AU PORTEUR

D'UNE ACTION DE QUATRE LIVRES STERLING

ENTIÈREMENT LIBÉRÉE

N° 82327

LE CAIRE, le 15 Novembre 1906

UN ADMINISTRATEUR

UN ADMINISTRATEUR

SOCIÉTÉ ANONYME DE WADI KOM-OMBO LE CAIRE EGYPTE

LITH. I. DELLA ROCCA - ALEX.

But with the heightening of the Aswan Reservoir, a second generation of sugar factories expanded across Upper Egypt including an important one in Kom-Ombo, a village north of Aswan bordering the (Ernest) Cassel irrigation canal.

With the availability of year-round water, Kom-Ombo, so far only known for its Ancient Egyptian temples, quickly turned into a thriving company town where its able bodied men, women and children worked for or became connected to the sugar industry.

Beside its fantastic turnaround from a forgotten village with old relics to a thriving crop producing center, Kom-Ombo became an issue with those who saw things otherwise. Conceived and created by an international group of Jewish capitalists, editorials came out referring to Kom-Ombo as an "Israeli Colony on Egyptian soil." Al-Ahram, in its editorial of 10 December 1903 went as far as saying that the Upper Egypt town was about to replicate of what was going on in Palestine.

"Once the Kom-Ombo plan is up and running, its owners plan to import Zionist laborers to till the land, similar to what Rothschild did in Palestine. Hence, Zionists need no longer go to Eastern Uganda as suggested by the British."

Under a regime of laisser-faire and with the blessings of both company chairman Youssef Cattaui Pasha and his deputy Talaat Harb Pasha, Egypt's sugar affairs were left entirely in the hands of the Belgian Henri Naus Bey.

From his smart office on Cairo's Sheik Abou al-Sebaa Street, the diminutive Belgian ran the Societe Generale des Sucreries et de la Raffinerie d'Égypte almost single-handedly from 1902 or thereabouts until he died in 1938. It was also thanks to Henri Naus and his Belgian associate Albert Ceyssens that the old Jamaican cane imported in the days of Viceroy Ibrahim Pasha (r. 1848) was replaced with the superior Javanese POJ 105 variety.

It was no coincidence that the owners of the Sugar Company were also the principal shareholders of the agricultural concerns that operated and managed Upper Egypt's vast sugar plantations. One of these mammoth concerns was the Wadi Kom-Ombo Company, the brainchild in 1904 of Sir Ernest Cassel of London, the same man who, in 1898, had heavily invested in the construction of the Aswan Reservoir.

Cassel's associates in Egypt included Raphael Suarès, Sir Elwin Palmer of the National Bank of Egypt, Sir Victor Harari Pasha of the Ministry of Finance, agronomist Victor Mosseri Bey, engineer Youssef Cattaui Pasha and banker Robert Rolo (later Sir Rolo). It was Sir Victor, who upon retiring from his government job in 1905, oversaw the new company's financial affairs.

Shortlisted to run the operations of the Wadi Kom-Ombo Land Reclamation Company was the capable Ismail Sirry Pasha who politely declined the offer. Hence the choice fell on Daira Sanieh Inspector General Birch Pasha who upon dying in January 1913 was replaced by Ahmed Moustafa Bey.

Société Fonciere du Domain du Cheikh Fadl

Registered on March 6, 1905 to acquire and develop the Sheikh Fadl Estate in Minia Province, Upper Egypt.

As of December 31, 1945, the company owned 7,000 feddans of agricultural land, with sugar-cane, cotton, wheat, barley, beans and maize as the principal crops.

The sugar factory at Sheikh Fadl gets all its supply of cane from the Sheikh Fadl Company.

Head Office: 8 Talaat Harb Pasha St (ex Sheikh Aboul Sebaa), Cairo.

Capital:
L.E. 779,500 divided into 194,875 Ordinary shares of L.E. 4 each, fully paid.

5 ACTIONS 20

Titre N° 023151

Société Foncière du Domaine de Cheikh Fadl

SOCIÉTÉ ANONYME

Autorisée par décret de S.A. le Khédive d'Egypte, en date du 6 Mars 1905 constituée le 21 Mars 1905

STATUTS DÉPOSÉS AU GREFFE COMMERCIAL DU TRIBUNAL MIXTE DU CAIRE LE 28 MARS 1905, SUB N° 99

MODIFIÉS PAR DECISIONS DE L'ASSEMBLÉE GÉNÉRALE EXTRAORDINAIRE DU 24 FÉVRIER 1938

CAPITAL SOCIAL L.E. 623600

DIVISE EN 155.900 ACTIONS DE LIVRES EGYPTIENNES 4 CHACUNE

SIÈGE SOCIAL AU CAIRE

TITRE AU PORTEUR DE CINQ ACTIONS DE L.Eg. 4

N° 035751 à N° 035755

Le Caire le 1er Mars 1938

UN ADMINISTRATEUR

UN ADMINISTRATEUR

SOCIÉTÉ FONCIÈRE DU DOMAINE DE CHEIKH FADL — SIÈGE SOCIAL AU CAIRE

١٨ ديسمبر سنة ١٩٥٤.

هذا السند خاضع للتخفيض

Société Foncière du Domaine de Cheikh Fadl
Le capital social a été réduit à L.E. 698400 divisé en 174.600 actions d'une valeur nominale de L.E. 4.— chacune, après amortissement de: 875 actions selon décision de l'Assemblée Générale Extraordinaire du ... et ... selon décision de l'Assemblée Générale Extraordinaire du 18 Décembre 1954.
Ce titre est soumis à la réduction indiquée ci-dessus.

LITHO. FLLI. VENTURA, ALEX.

SOCIÉTÉ FONCIÈRE DU DOMAINE DE CHEIKH FADL 50 Titre N° 023151 50 DE CINQ ACTIONS N° 035751 A N° 035755 COUPON PAYABLE AU PORTEUR	SOCIÉTÉ FONCIÈRE DU DOMAINE DE CHEIKH FADL 49 Titre N° 023151 49 DE CINQ ACTIONS N° 035751 A N° 035755 COUPON PAYABLE AU PORTEUR	SOCIÉTÉ FONCIÈRE DU DOMAINE DE CHEIKH FADL 48 Titre N° 023151 48 DE CINQ ACTIONS N° 035751 A N° 035755 COUPON PAYABLE AU PORTEUR	SOCIÉTÉ FONCIÈRE DU DOMAINE DE CHEIKH FADL 47 Titre N° 023151 47 DE CINQ ACTIONS N° 035751 A N° 035755 COUPON PAYABLE AU PORTEUR	SOCIÉTÉ FONCIÈRE DU DOMAINE DE CHEIKH FADL 46 Titre N° 023151 46 DE CINQ ACTIONS N° 035751 A N° 035755 COUPON PAYABLE AU PORTEUR

A self-made agronomist, Ahmed Moustafa Bey had allegedly started out as the nazir (superintendent) of his grandfather's (Hassan Sharkass Pasha) estates. Brimming with experience, the Wadi Kom-Ombo Company entrusted him with the management of thirty thousand feddans *taftish*, much of it allocated to a new sugar cane variety. Henceforth Ahmed Mustafa would be referred to as al-Mufatish.

Having become a virtual company town with Ahmed Moustafa Bey in charge of the Kom-Ombo Company's Agricultural Division, Kom-Ombo's Mufatish was regarded by the fellahin (peasants) as their de facto employer and paymaster. And as if his already heavy charge were not enough, each year, during cane sowing and harvesting seasons, Moustafa's manpower would quadruple in size. This also meant wages had to be renegotiated and special cash payments handled.

But the season of 1919 would be different and the Mufatish was confronted with much more than he had bargained for.

Despite all the trappings of statehood — ceremonial head of state, council of ministers, flag, customs and postal administration — Egypt in 1919 remained a virtual British colony or protectorate. All civil servants, from the Sultan down to the smallest army officer, were ultimately accountable to Lord Allenby, the fearless British High Commissioner. If the Mufatish was considered Kom-Ombo's paymaster by the local peasantry, Lord Allenby was regarded by most Egyptians as the nation's paymaster even if Egypt invariably retained its own national currency.

Historians agree that the events of 1919 ultimately brought Egypt a measure of independence. It was also that year that Egyptians discovered Saad Zaghloul, a candid patriotic man who stood up to British oppression and publicly opposed its policies.

Behind the fiery, old pasha rallied an entire population.

But instead of hearing out the nationalists and negotiating a settlement with the pasha, the British High Commissioner, on 8 March 1919, deported Zaghloul and his senior backers — Ismail Sidky Pasha and Mohammed Mahmoud Pasha (all three future prime ministers of Egypt) — to Malta. Lord Allenby was not tolerating any independist talk.

Within days, Egypt flared up in an unprecedented revolt resulting in a total breakdown of vital transport and communication system with a near crippling effect on the nation's economy. Railway lines were torn up, stations burned, telephone and telegraph wires cut. This was followed with a general strike by Egyptian officials and the resignation of the Egyptian government.

The paralysis was complete. Cairo was isolated from the rest of the country. For the first time British high-handedness had not paid off and Zaghloul was released on 7 April 1919.

As far as the British High Commissioner and his advisors were concerned, the time had come to re-assess the

Société Anonyme du Chemin de Fer Keneh–Assouan

Registered on July 6, 1895 to acquire a concession from the Egyptian Government for the construction of a railway in Upper Egypt. The 80-year concession was to expire in 1980.

The railway had a total length of 270 kilometres. From its completion in 1900, the line was leased to the Egyptian Government for the duration of the concession against an annual payment: L.E. 24,750 since 1921, and variable prior to that. The Egyptian Government decided to purchase the undertaking and the company went into liquidation on January 2nd, 1948. The purchase price was L.E. 448,484.

Liquidation and Distribution of assets:
Surplus assets remaining after the return of the whole of the paid-up capital were be distributed as follows:
–15% proportionately divided among holders of the 500 Founders shares.
–85% proportionately divided among the holders of the 5,000 Jouissance shares.

Head Office: 14 Talaat Harb Pasha Street, Cairo.

Capital:
5,000 Jouissance share of no par value.
500 Founders shares of no par value.

Société Anonyme du Chemin de Fer Keneh Assouan

Autorisée par décret de S.A. le Khédive d'Egypte
en date du 6 Juillet 1895

Siège Social au Caire

CAPITAL LIVRES STERLING 100,000

PART DE FONDATION
au Porteur

N°

Le Caire, le 19 Juillet 1895

Un Administrateur

L'Administrateur Délégué

SOCIÉTÉ ANONYME DU CHEMIN DE FER KENEH ASSOUAN
CAIRE
EGYPTE

damage, pick up the pieces and restore a new modus vivendi. But first, there were accounts to be settled. One of them was in Kom-Ombo.

Summer comes earlier in Upper Egypt than it does in Lower Egypt. Hence it is not unusual that a crop is attended to in the south several weeks before it is in the Delta. A delay of a few days could jeopardize an entire yield. The outbreak of the March 1919 events, coinciding with sowing time in Kom-Ombo, placed the entire harvest and the Mufatish in dire straits.

For several days Kom-Ombo had been cut off from the company's head office. The small branch of the National Bank of Egypt which served Kom-Ombo was out of funds and new cash shipments were improbable as no trains arrived from Cairo. As a result, liquidity had dried up and hoarding had begun in earnest across Kom-Ombo and its dependencies. The Mufatish was faced with a dilemma of untold proportions. If he did not pay his inflated labor force there would be no harvesting that year.

No harvest meant Egypt's sugar factories would come to a grinding halt and a whole year's yield would perish. Barter was out of question. Even Kom-Ombo had subscribed to 20th century practices and was not about to revert to bartering tribal beads for kilos of grains. The only feasible alternative for the Mufatish was to print his own money. A daring move since no comparable precedent existed in Egypt's modern history. Even Mohammed Ali Pasha had abstained from such a move fearing his sovereign in Constantinople.

Ahmed Moustafa Bey's money was a rudimentary affair. No coins, just plain-cut paper bearing a simple handwritten inscription promising to pay the bearer the shown amount upon demand. It was signed by the Mufatish. The five, ten, fifty piastre denominations as well as the one, five and ten pound notes were neither backed by gold or silver, nor were they convertible into any known legal tender. The only cover was Ahmed Moustafa Bey's integrity and the standing he enjoyed in Kom-Ombo. The fellahin, the migrant laborers, the tradesmen and the civil servants agreed to go along.

Once the new money was circulated, the sugar cane crop was saved and the sugar factories were ensured their quota of raw material. The Mufatish who already represented law and order for the entire area had proved his mettle. Kom-Ombo had become an autonomous mini republic.

The implication of Ahmed Moustafa Bey's resolve was not lost on the British. Here was an independent spirit capable of pragmatic solutions. Translated into colonial jargon, 'a dangerous subversive mind had resolved a complex situation,' qualities the foreign occupier could not appreciate in others but himself. The revolutionary Mufatish had to be taught a lesson for his ingenuity, or impunity if you wish.

Even before alleged accusations started to pour in, Ahmed Moustafa Bey was arrested. Charges ranged from his ordering the interruption of the railway service in his area to harboring subversive elements. Under the prevailing martial law, the Mufatish was guilty of high treason deserving capital punishment.

Travaux d'Irrigation du Gouvernement Égyptien

In 1898-9, the Egyptian Government, in shortage of funds to finance the building of the Aswan and Assiut dams, reached a deal between its Ministry of Public Works and the contracting company, the British firm John Aird & Co., whereby the government committed to settle on 1 January 1927 the sum of 500 sterling pounds for each of these "mandat de paiement" whether it be to the company proper or to individual bearers. However, any mandats, with serial numbers 158 or above will only be owed 137 sterling pounds each.

The hidden key player in this deal was Sir Ernest Cassel who also had an instrumental role in the dealings of the Daira Sanieh. Behind the scenes, the firm of John Aird & Co. had signed a contract with Sir Ernest Cassel's Irrigation Investment Corporation Ltd. to finance Aird's Aswan and Assiut barrages construction works. Other than the interest reaped on this deal, the construction of the barrages would enable Cassel's company to reclaim thousands of new acres south of Kom-Ombo and to skyrocket the value of the Daira Sanieh shares and lands.

Numéro de Série 48

Numéro d'Ordre 65

TRAVAUX D'IRRIGATION DU GOUVERNEMENT ÉGYPTIEN

ASSOUAN ET ASSIOUT 1898

£500 STERLING.

MANDAT DE PAIEMENT

£500 STERLING.

Le Gouvernement Égyptien déclare par les présentes, qu'en retour de travaux effectués et de matériaux fournis pour les travaux d'irrigation susmentionnés, *il reconnaît devoir,* absolument, et sans condition aucune, à MM. JOHN AIRD et CIE, la somme de **Cinq cents livres sterling (£500).**

Le Gouvernement s'engage par les présentes à payer à MM. JOHN AIRD et CIE, ou au PORTEUR DE CE MANDAT, le **Ier Janvier 1927** la dite somme de **Cinq cents livres sterling.**

Ce paiement s'effectuera à **LONDRES,** par l'intermédiare de la Banque d'Angleterre, contre la remise de ce mandat.

Ce paiement sera effectué à tout événement AU PORTEUR des présentes, en totalité et sans déduction quelconque et indépendamment de toute contestation qui peut être actuellement pendante ou qui pourrait s'élever dans la suite entre le Gouvernement et MM. John Aird et Cie, ou de toute autre contestation quelle qu'elle soit, la dette reconnue par les présentes étant pour une somme certaine et déterminée et constituant une créance liquide et reconnue par le Gouvernement Égyptien.

Le présent mandat confère au porteur, jusqu'à son entier désintéressement, une affectation sur les travaux pour assurer le paiement de la somme indiquée dans ce mandat, et le dit porteur pourra, d'accord avec les porteurs de tous autres mandats émis par rapport aux mêmes travaux (dont le maximum ne devra pas toutefois excéder les limites mentionnées dans la table au dos des présentes) ou d'accord avec la majorité de ces porteurs, nommer ou faire nommer par l'autorité compétente un représentant chargé de mettre à exécution de la manière qu'il appartiendra le dit droit d'affectation, au cas où ce mandat n'aura pas été payé à l'échéance.

Aucune prise de possession par le Gouvernement des travaux ni aucun autre acte quelconque ne seront susceptibles de porter atteinte à la dite affectation.

Le présent mandat et tous autres mandats émis ou à émettre dans les limites susmentionnées auront rang égal et *pari passu* sans aucun droit de préférence ni de priorité à raison de leur numéro, série, date d'émission ou autre circonstance quelconque.

En date du 10 Octobre 1899

Pour le Gouvernement,

Le Ministre des Travaux Publics.

H. Fakhry

Contresigné

Ingénieur du Gouvernement Egyptien.

W. Garstin

Imp. A. P. Blundell, Taylor & Cie 173, Upper Thames St Londres.

Ahmed Moustafa Bey remained imperturbable, confidant that a harsh sentence would trigger spontaneous uprising from Kom-Ombo to Aswan. Moreover, the company's powerful Jewish shareholders, brought considerable pressure on London so that the Mufatish's death sentence was commuted. The farsighted company directors were only too keen to have the man who had proved his metal in times of crisis reinstated.

It came as no surprise when three years later, the Mufatish was designated senator for the district of Kom-Ombo at the inauguration of Egypt's first constitutional parliament during King Fouad's reign. The nationalists had won.

Meanwhile, Ahmed Mustafa Bey's celebrated banknotes were gradually retired from the market in exchange for National Bank of Egypt legal tender. The few specimens that survived are coveted collectors' items appearing from time to time at Christie's of London or Sotheby's in New York.

Today, for the non-numismatics, the Mufatish notes represent an important milestone in Egypt's modern history. Senator Ahmed Moustafa Bey's tangible initiative and his ephemeral republic of Kom-Ombo are testimonials that in days gone by, public administrators had the guts to take action.

La Fluviale

La Fluvial S.A.E. was formed on May 14, 1938 and registered as an Egyptian limited company on December 27 of the same year. Its objectives were to continue the business of Nile navigation and building of river craft, formely carried on by "La Fluviale" F. van der Zee and Co., originally established on January 1, 1927.

The company had an agreement with the Societe Misr pour le Transport et la Navigation for the joint working of the fleets of the two companies on a half-share profit basis.

Head Office: 1 Cherif Pasha Street, Alexandria.

Capital:
L.E. 140,635 divided into 28,125 Ordinary shares of L.E. 5 each, fully paid.

لافلوڤيال
شركة مساهمة مصرية

5 ACTIONS *SÉRIE A* L.Eg. 25

LA FLUVIALE

SOCIÉTÉ ANONYME EGYPTIENNE
AUTORISÉE PAR DÉCRET ROYAL EN DATE DU 27 DÉCEMBRE 1938
INSCRITE AU REGISTRE DU COMMERCE À ALEXANDRIE SUB N° 18702

SIÈGE SOCIAL : ALEXANDRIE, EGYPTE

تنفيذا لقرار [illegible] المنعقدة بتاريخ
يونيو ١٩٦١ تقرر تخفيض رأس مال [illegible]
من مبلغ ١٣٥٠٠٠ جنيه الى ١٠٨٠٠٠ جنيه بواقع جنيه مصري
للسهم الواحد فتصير القيمة الاسمية للسهم اربعة جنيهات بدلا
من [illegible]

CAPITAL SOCIAL LIVRES EGYPTIENNES 135.000
DIVISÉ EN 27.000 ACTIONS DE L. EG. 5 CHACUNE

CINQ ACTIONS AU PORTEUR
entièrement libérées

N° 17746 À N° 17750

UN ADMINISTRATEUR UN ADMINISTRATEUR

ALEXANDRIE, le 11 Avril 1951

LA FLUVIALE
SOCIÉTÉ ANONYME EGYPTIENNE
CINQ ACTIONS

LA FLUVIALE
SOCIÉTÉ ANONYME EGYPTIENNE
CINQ ACTIONS

LA FLUVIALE
SOCIÉTÉ ANONYME EGYPTIENNE
CINQ ACTIONS

LA FLUVIALE
SOCIÉTÉ ANONYME EGYPTIENNE
CINQ ACTIONS

LA FLUVIALE
SOCIÉTÉ ANONYME EGYPTIENNE
CINQ ACTIONS

PAYE
Suivant décision de l'Assemblée Génér
Extraordinaire de la Société tenue le 22 Février 193
le présent titre au porteur a été converti en
nominatif et il a été créé pour le cas de toute cessi
ou mutation par décès au profit d'une perso
autre qu'un courtier inscrit à la Bourse des Vale
du Caire, un droit de préemption au profit
Le présent titre est inscrit dans
registres de la Société au nom de
Un administrateur
Par décision de l'Assem. Gén. Ex. du 28 Avril 1934 le Capital Social a été porté à L.Eg. 30.000, dont L.Eg. 22.000 émis et divisé en 4400 actions de L.Eg. 5 chacune
SOCIÉTÉ ANONYME DE L'IMMEUBLE DE LA BOURSE DU CAIRE
SOCIÉTÉ ANONYME EGYPTIENNE
Autorisée par Décret Royal du 16 Octobre 1926
SIÈGE SOCIAL - LE CAIRE (EGYPTE)
Capital L.E. 20.000 en 4000 actions de L.E. 5 chacune
PORTÉ A CE CHIFFRE SELON DÉCISION DE L'ASSEMBLÉE GÉNÉRALE EXTRAORDINAIRE DU 7 JUIN 1927
Suivant décision de l'Assemblée Générale Extraordinaire tenue le 25 Mars 1931, le droit de préemption, créé par l'Assemblée du 22 Février 1930, est exclusivement réservé aux Agents de Change inscrits à la Bourse des Valeurs du Caire et au Syndicat des Agents de Change du Caire.
UN ADMINISTRATEUR
1 ACTION
TITRE [redacted] NOMINATIF POUR
UNE ACTION DE L.EG. CINQ
5 L.E.
UN ADMINISTRATEUR
Nº 4212
Le Caire, le 7 Juin 1927
Le porteur du présent titre est propriétaire d'une Action entièrement libérée de la Société Anonyme de l'Immeuble de la Bourse du Caire portant le numéro ci-dessus et soumise aux prescriptions des Statuts de la Société et aux résolutions des assemblées générales
SOCIÉTÉ ANONYME DE L'IMMEUBLE DE LA BOURSE DU CAIRE
LE CAIRE